Great Masters:
Beethoven—His Life and Music
Robert Greenberg, Ph.D.

PUBLISHED BY:

THE TEACHING COMPANY
4840 Westfields Boulevard, Suite 500
Chantilly, Virginia 20151-2299
1-800-TEACH-12
Fax—703-378-3819
www.teach12.com

Acknowledgments begin on page 75 and constitute a continuation
of the copyright page.

Robert Greenberg, Ph.D.

Chairman, Department of Music History and Literature
San Francisco Conservatory of Music

Robert Greenberg has composed over forty works for a wide variety of instrumental and vocal ensembles. Recent performances of Greenberg's work have taken place in New York, San Francisco, Los Angeles, Chicago, England, Ireland, Italy, Greece, and The Netherlands, where his *Child's Play* for string quartet was performed at the Concertgebouw of Amsterdam.

Professor Greenberg holds degrees from Princeton University and the University of California at Berkeley, where he received a Ph.D. in music composition in 1984. His principal teachers were Edward Cone, Claudio Spies, Andrew Imbrie, and Olly Wilson.

Professor Greenberg's awards include three Nicola De Lorenzo prizes in composition, three Meet the Composer grants, and commissions from the Koussevitzky Foundation of the Library of Congress, the Alexander String Quartet, XTET, the San Francisco Contemporary Music Players, and the Dancer's Stage Ballet Company.

He is currently on the faculty of the San Francisco Conservatory of Music, where he served as Chair of the Department of Music History and Literature and Director of Curriculum of the Adult Extension Division for thirteen years.

Professor Greenberg is resident music historian for National Public Radio's "Weekend All Things Considered" program. He has taught and lectured extensively across North America and Europe, speaking to such corporations and musical institutions as Arthur Andersen and Andersen Consulting, Harvard Business School Publishing, Deutches Financial Services, Canadian Pacific, Strategos Institute, Lincoln Center, the Van Cliburn Foundation, the University of California/Haas School of Business Executive Seminar, the University of Chicago Graduate School of Business, the Chautauqua Institute, the Commonwealth Club of San Francisco, and others. His work as a teacher and lecturer has been profiled in the *Wall Street Journal, Inc.* magazine, the *San Francisco Chronicle*, and *The Times* of London. He is an artistic codirector and board member of COMPOSER, INC. His music is published by Fallen Leaf Press and CPP/Belwin and is recorded on the Innova Label.

Table of Contents
Great Masters:
Beethoven—His Life and Music

Great Masters: Beethoven—His Life and Music

Scope:

Ludwig van Beethoven experienced "rebirth" as an artist three times over the course of his life. He was born on December 17, 1770, into what we would call today a dysfunctional family, with an abusive and alcoholic father and a depressed mother. His musical talent was recognized early, but his father attempted to beat him into becoming a child prodigy to rival Mozart. It was a futile attempt; there could only be one Mozart. By 1785, the young Beethoven was the sole breadwinner for the family and, in 1787, the primary caregiver for his younger brothers. In 1789, he sought and was granted some relief from these responsibilities from local authorities and experienced his first musical rebirth. During this period of intense composition, Beethoven wrote five sets of piano variations, ballet music, concert arias, chamber works for piano and winds, and two cantatas for vocal soloists, chorus, and orchestra.

When he moved to Vienna to study with Haydn in 1792, Beethoven earned a reputation as an outstanding pianist and, as a pianist, became the darling of the Austro-Hungarian aristocracy. These early years in Vienna were also significant for his compositional career. From 1792–1803, he produced, among many other works, the Opus 1 Trios for Piano, Violin, and 'Cello; the Opus 18 string quartets, and the Symphony No. 1 in C Major. In 1801, Beethoven's career and finances were flourishing, but he was in poor health. His hearing loss was becoming progressively worse, and Beethoven grew increasingly depressed and panicked about it. His emotional crisis came to a head in 1802, but served as the creative catharsis for his second rebirth in 1803, in a self-sufficient and heroic guise.

In 1802, Beethoven was poised to reinvent himself as a hero, struggling against his fate. His "model" for this new self-image was Napoleon Bonaparte, who at the time, represented a vision of individualism and empowerment. Beethoven's music reflects this vision in its insistence on expressing the heights and depths of the artist's emotions. His Symphony No. 3 in Eb Major, Op. 55, for example, was nothing less than revolutionary in its grand proportions and dramatic expressive content. This first of the so-called "Heroic Symphonies" changed the history of Western music. During this so-called "Heroic" compositional period, from 1803–1812, Beethoven produced such masterworks as the Fourth, Fifth, Sixth,

Seventh, and Eighth Symphonies; the five middle string quartets; the Mass in C Major; and the opera *Fidelio*. Toward the end of this period, however, Beethoven experienced a short-lived affair with the "Immortal Beloved," which ultimately precipitated his fall into four years of despair, destruction of his brother's remaining family, and public ridicule.

In 1819, Beethoven used these events, once again, as a catalyst for an artistic rebirth. In the last years of his life, he wrote many of his greatest, most profound, and most "modern" works, including the six late string quartets, the Ninth Symphony, and *Missa Solemnis*. Indeed, Beethoven's Symphony No. 9 became the single most influential piece of music composed in the 19th century. The work breaks with time-honored conventions and distinctions to give precedence to the expressive needs and desires of the artist. During these last years, Beethoven was consumed by his craft but still difficult with friends, family, and business associates. He died on March 26, 1827, having reconciled himself somewhat with his family, and was given a loving tribute by the people of Vienna.

Lecture One
The Immortal Beloved

Scope: Perhaps Beethoven's foremost physical characteristic was his hair. Heinrich Friedrich Ludwig Rellstab, a journalist, music critic, and contemporary of Beethoven's described his hair as: "Not frizzy, not straight, but a mixture of everything." (Incidentally, it was Rellstab who first referred to Beethoven's Piano Sonata Op. 27, No. 2, in terms of "moonlight." **Musical selection at piano**: Piano Sonata No. 14 in C# Minor, Op. 27, No. 2, movement 1 [1801].) Beethoven's hair is now back in the news. Eight strands of it were studied for four years, and the study revealed that the hairs contained, on average, a lead concentration of sixty parts per million. According to this research, that amount is more than enough to cause the abdominal distress, irritability, and depression that Beethoven suffered from for most of his adult life. Although scientists doubt that lead poisoning contributed to his deafness, more research will also be conducted in that area.

Beethoven, however, also exhibited a pathological hatred for authority, a persecution complex, and delusional behaviors, which cannot be attributed to lead poisoning. These physical, emotional, and spiritual problems were the result of a lifetime of struggle and frustration, which forced him to look inward and reinvent himself and, in so doing, reinvent the nature of musical expression in the Western world.

Outline

I. In December 1813, Ludwig van Beethoven—almost forty-three years old—was once again at the top of the Viennese musical world. He had made one of the great comebacks of all time.

   A. In December 1813, Beethoven's Seventh Symphony was premiered to great acclaim; the second movement of the Seventh was so popular that it was routinely repeated in performances of the symphony, inserted into other of Beethoven's symphonies, and even performed as a self-standing composition. (**Musical**

selection: Symphony No. 7 in A Major, Op. 92, movement 2 [1812].)

B. In 1814, Beethoven's opera *Fidelio* was finally performed, to ecstatic audience response.

C. He was also acclaimed as a hero of the Austrian nation, because he had co-written *Wellington's Victory*, a piece of music that celebrated Wellington's victory over a Napoleonic army at the Battle of Vittoria, in Spain, in 1813. This piece was premiered just as Napoleon's reign of terror was coming to an end.

D. According to some sources, Beethoven made more money between late 1813 and early 1815 than during the rest of his career all together.

E. His fall from grace, then, in 1815 was that much more terrifying for the height from which he fell. His compositional muse abandoned him almost entirely; he became embroiled in a legal dispute that would cost him most of his savings and a good bit of his sanity; and he was soon to become clinically deaf.

F. Yet, after four years of living in despair; after destroying the lives of his sister-in-law Johanna and her son; his hearing finally gone; some of his most cherished delusions held up to public ridicule, Beethoven would—in about 1819—reinvent himself for the third time in his life.

    1. In the last seven years of his life, Beethoven would write his greatest, most profound, and most forward-looking works.

    2. These works include the *Diabelli Variations*, the late Piano Sonatas, the six late string quartets, the Ninth Symphony, and the *Missa Solemnis*. (**Musical selection**: *Missa Solemnis* in D Major, Op. 123, Gloria [1823].)

G. We are left with significant questions:

    1. What precipitated Beethoven's fall from popular grace in 1815?

    2. What was Beethoven's problem with his sister-in-law Johanna, and why did he feel he had the right to wrest his nephew Karl away from his mother?

    3. Why was Beethoven willing to gamble his financial and emotional well-being on such a protracted and ugly legal battle?

    4. What were the delusions that were scuttled in the years between 1815 and 1819, and how did their destruction allow Beethoven to free himself of emotional baggage that otherwise might have meant the end of his compositional career?

    5. Why was Beethoven so difficult?

II. Beethoven was an angry, frustrated man of genius living in an age of violent change.

    A. He grew up in a violently dysfunctional family.

    B. He was a survivor, a fighter, an egotist who knew his worth in an age of patronage, a man whose personal self-identification with the great warrior/hero/monster of the age—Napoleon Bonaparte—bordered on the pathological.

    C. Slowly and painfully, over a period of twenty-two years, Beethoven—composer, virtuoso pianist, man of music—went deaf.

    D. He was also terribly unlucky in love.

        1. Beethoven's disastrous love life precipitated the personal and legal crises of 1815–1819 more than any other single event.

        2. In April 1812, Beethoven was forty-one years old. He had completed the brilliant Symphony No. 7, his so-called "dance symphony," a piece of music that reveals a composer at the very top of his game. (**Musical selection**: Symphony No. 7 in A Major, Op. 92, movement 4, conclusion.)

        3. The brilliant, joyful surface of this music belies a composer in the throes of romantic despair. Beethoven was in love, and he knew it could not end well.

III. Before we can discuss the events surrounding Beethoven in 1812, we must first examine Beethoven's attitudes toward women, love, and marriage and women's attitudes toward Beethoven.

    A. Beethoven was constantly falling in love with unattainable women.

        1. Before he moved to Vienna, at age twenty-two in 1792, Beethoven's first great loves were women who were both engaged to be married.

        2. His first crush in Vienna was on a singer named Magdalena Willmann. Beethoven was so smitten by Magdalena that he apparently proposed to her one day out of the blue. She rejected Beethoven's proposal out of hand, telling him, according to biographer Alexander Thayer, that he was "ugly and half crazy."

B. Although many women were initially attracted to Beethoven, they were quickly turned off by his shabby and uncouth appearance and behavior and his almost complete lack of social graces.

C. Beethoven's attitude toward marriage was conditioned by the dreadful example of his parents' marriage.

IV. Beethoven was born in the Rhineland city of Bonn on December 17, 1770. Three adults in his early life shaped his view of marriage, parenthood, and domestic life: his paternal grandfather, his father, and his mother.

   A. Beethoven was named for his paternal grandfather. The elder Beethoven was the first musician in the family, a singer, and Kapellmeister at the Electoral Court in Bonn. He was an important, respected, and talented man, a patriarchal character with a domineering personality.

      1. Born in 1712 in Flanders, in Belgium, Beethoven's grandfather died on December 24, 1773, when Ludwig was but three years old. Despite the fact that Ludwig hardly knew him, the composer maintained a lifelong reverence for his grandfather.

      2. Beethoven's grandfather married Maria Josepha Poll. Maria Josepha was an alcoholic, and as a result, she was placed in a cloister for at least the last fifteen years of her life. The de facto breakup up of his marriage because of his wife's alcoholism left Beethoven's grandfather bereft.

      3. There is no evidence that the elder Beethoven ever again had a relationship with a woman; he remained alone in his flat with his one surviving child, his son (and Beethoven's father), Johann.

   B. Johann van Beethoven, born in 1739 or 1740, was the only one of his parents' three children to survive his childhood. He was a tenor and music teacher at the Elector's Court. He was a weak man with a weak personality, overshadowed and psychologically abused by his father.

1. Ludwig, Sr., told anyone who would listen that his son, Johann, would never amount to anything.
2. Despite these feelings, Ludwig, Sr., had no intention of sharing Johann with anyone, particularly a woman. Ludwig, Sr., was enraged when, in 1767, the twenty-seven-year-old Johann announced his desire to wed Maria Magdelena Keverich Leym, a childless widow of twenty-one.
3. Johann van Beethoven's marriage to Maria Magdalena was perhaps the only important thing he ever did in his life without his father's approval.

C. For her part, Maria Magdalena van Beethoven, the third major influence in Beethoven's childhood, was depressed and disillusioned by her marriage to a weak, abusive alcoholic.
1. One biographer, Maynard Solomon, wrote:

> Maria Magdelena assumed the role of the pained, suffering, righteous wife of a ne'er-do-well drunkard and played it in high, tragic style. Cacilia Fischer could not remember ever having seen Frau van Beethoven laugh ("She was always serious"), and the widow Karth described her as "a quiet, suffering woman."

2. Solomon goes on to say that Maria probably passed her cheerless outlook onto her children, including her notion that marriage is "A little joy, followed by a chain of sorrows."

D. What was the influence of all of these people on the sensitive and impressionable young Beethoven?
1. He viewed his mother as a martyr.
2. He may have learned that marriage is a "trap."
3. He saw his grandfather as the true man of the family.
4. He chose not to be his father's son.

E. Despite this view of marriage and family, by the age of forty (in about 1810), part of Ludwig van Beethoven wanted to settle down.
1. He yearned for the sort of security and affection he believed (or at least hoped!) that marriage could bring.
2. He was also aware that his desire to marry was not compatible with his dedication to music.

V. Love, marriage, and love lost were very much on Beethoven's mind during the years 1812 and 1813—the year of and the year following the affair that we now know as the "Immortal Beloved."

   A. Among the papers that Beethoven left after his death was a long love letter, filled with spontaneity, passion, exaltation, confusion, and frankly conflicting emotions. The letter clearly shows that Beethoven—probably for the first and only time in his life—had fallen passionately in love with a woman who felt the same way about him.

   1. The letter is dated only July 6 and 7; there is no year in the date.

   2. Nowhere does the letter say to whom it is addressed.

   3. The speculation and controversy as to who was the Immortal Beloved went on for over 150 years.

   4. Thanks to Maynard Solomon and some extraordinary scholarship, we now know that the date of the Immortal Beloved letter was July 6 and 7, 1812, and its recipient was Antonie Brentano.

   5. Antonie, or "Toni" von Birkenstock was born in Vienna of the nobility in 1780; she was ten years Beethoven's junior.

   6. In 1798, at age eighteen, she moved to Frankfurt, having married Franz Brentano, a prominent merchant and banker from that city. He was thirty-three, fifteen years her senior.

   7. Antonie met Beethoven in May of 1810 when she accompanied her sister-in-law on a visit to the composer. A close friendship developed between Antonie and Beethoven over the next two years.

   B. What happened between Antonie and Ludwig?

   1. Antonie's relationship with her husband, Franz Brentano, was warm and affectionate, but there is no evidence that it was ever a marriage of love or passion.

   2. The worst part of her marriage, for Antonie, was having to leave her beloved Vienna and move to Frankfurt—a city she came to detest for its lack of culture and provincialism. When her father died in 1809, Antonie returned to Vienna, ostensibly to settle his estate, and managed to prolong her stay there for three years.

3. By early 1812, when it became apparent that she would soon have to return to Frankfurt, she became clinically depressed and began suffering psychosomatic symptoms. She withdrew almost entirely from all visitors, except Beethoven.
4. Despite the fact that she was a married mother of four and of aristocratic birth, it now appears likely that sometime around July 3, 1812, Antonie Brentano offered to leave her husband and children and remain in Vienna with Beethoven.
5. The lovers arranged to rendezvous in Bohemia a few days later; it was from Bohemia that Beethoven wrote the Immortal Beloved letter, on July 6 and 7, 1812.

C. Probably the last thing that Beethoven ever expected was to have his love so unequivocally reciprocated. His letter is filled with confusion and ambivalence.
1. Even as he professed his eternal, undying love to Antonie Brentano, Beethoven was equivocating. He knew full well that he was incapable of the sort of life that Antonie had offered him.
2. Beethoven broke off the relationship. Maynard Solomon writes:

    > Beethoven understood that for one moment of his life he had within his grasp a woman's unconditional love. [But] Beethoven could not overcome the nightmarish burden of his past and set the ghosts to rest. His only hope was that somehow he could make Antonie understand (as he himself did not) the implacable barrier to their union without at the same time losing her love. (Solomon, p. 246)

3. The end of his affair with Antonie Brentano devastated Beethoven and would profoundly affect and shape the remaining fifteen years of his life.

Lecture Two
What Comes down Must Go up, 1813–1815

Scope: In the summer of 1812, after the Immortal Beloved affair, Beethoven composed one of his most upbeat pieces of music, the Symphony No. 8 in F Major, Op. 83. On its surface, the symphony seems to be in the classical style, but it is filled with quite modern twists and turns. Beethoven may have conceived this humorous piece as a kind of antidote to his depression over the relationship with Antonie Brentano and his worsening hearing. In November and December 1812, Beethoven composed his Sonata for Violin and Piano in G Major, Op. 96, after which his mental and physical health deteriorated. He fell into a deepening depression in the winter of 1812–1813 and composed nothing of significance. In the summer of 1813, he was approached by a friend to write a piece of music commemorating Wellington's defeat of one of Napoleon's armies. When it premiered in December of 1813, this piece, *Wellington's Victory* was an overwhelming success, garnering Beethoven a new level of popularity.

Outline

I. Having ended his relationship with Antonie Brentano in July 1812, Beethoven did his best to settle back into a creative routine.

   A. At first, he managed to succeed; the Immortal Beloved affair and its conclusion correspond exactly with the composition of the brilliant, humorous, and upbeat Symphony No. 8 in F Major, Op. 93, composed between April and August 1812.

      1. Actually, the upbeat nature of the Eighth betrays Beethoven's dark mood; he wrote much of his most brilliant and upbeat music—Symphonies Nos. 2, 7, and 8, for example—when he was most unhappy and depressed, even marginally suicidal.

      2. The therapeutic benefit of writing music that would help lift him out of his funk was preferable to writing music that mirrored and, perhaps, intensified his unhappiness.

   B. Clearly, in the late summer and fall of 1812, Beethoven needed these therapeutic benefits. Aside from his deepening depression over the outcome of the Immortal Beloved affair, his hearing took a turn for the worse.

II. The Eighth Symphony was the last symphony Beethoven would compose for ten years.

    A. On its surface, it seems to be a throwback to the symphonic style of Haydn, an "homage" to such classical-era ideals as clarity, lightness, wit, and expressive restraint. In reality, the Eighth is filled with extraordinary and modern musical turns and expressive twists.

    B. For example, in the beginning of the first movement, Beethoven comes directly to the point with a bright, compact theme that begins without any introduction. On the surface, this straight-arrow tune could have been written by Haydn himself. (**Musical selection**: Symphony No. 8 in F Major, Op. 93, movement 1, theme 1 [1812].)

        1. The twist is in the phrase structure. If Haydn had written this theme, we would have heard two balanced phrases, what we call an antecedent-consequent phrase structure.

        2. But Beethoven does not use that structure. Despite its classical melodic character and brevity, this theme features a very interesting and unusual structure of three phrases, antecedent-antecedent-consequent. (**Musical selection**: Symphony No. 8 in F Major, Op. 93, movement 1, theme 1.)

        3. Later in the movement, when this opening theme makes its *fortississimo* (*fff*) return, Beethoven shows his awareness of our knowledge that the three-phrase structure was unusual: When the theme returns in the low strings and bassoons, it is compressed into two phrases—the classical-era/textbook phrase structure that we "expected" all along!

        4. Immediately following this explosive two-phrase version of the theme, Beethoven slyly and quietly offers us the complete three-phrase version.

        5. Listen to this moment of the movement: the triumphant two-phrase version, followed immediately by the quiet three-phrase version. (**Musical selection**: Symphony No. 8 in F Major, Op. 93, movement 1, theme 1, recapitulation.)

    C. In lieu of a traditional slow movement, the second movement of Beethoven's Eighth is, instead, a comic tribute to the metronome—a newfangled device traditionally (but erroneously) attributed to Beethoven's friend Johann Nepomuk Malzel.

1. The metronome's exact, merciless ticking forces musicians to play mechanically. Yet the metronome is irreplaceable for establishing the proper speed (tempo) of a given piece of music and for learning to play with a steady beat. Beethoven's Eighth Symphony describes the musician's love/hate relationship with the metronome.

2. A brief but telling introduction describes the device. We hear metronomic ticking that in performance will be played by winds and horns. (**Musical selection at the piano**: Symphony No. 8 in F Major, Op. 93, movement 2, introduction.)

3. A stiff, almost cartoon-like theme grows out of the ticking introduction; the melody is as mechanical as the device that rules it. As the theme progresses, we hear a number of sudden and disturbing accents, or "syncopations," where they don't belong; the "theme" is having trouble following the ticking of the accompaniment! (**Musical selection**: Symphony No. 8 in F Major, Op. 93, movement 2, introduction and theme A, ms. 1–20.)

4. We even hear some moments when the metronome portrayed by the accompaniment needs to be wound up. (**Musical selection**: Symphony No. 8 in F Major, Op. 93, movement 2, ms. 20–25.)

5. The conclusion of the movement is pure cartoon music! The metronome dies and, with it, the patience of its user. (**Musical selection**: Symphony No. 8 in F Major, Op. 93, movement 2, coda.)

D. The third movement of Beethoven's Eighth is a quirky minuet and the fourth is a banquet of slapstick musical humor. Although the Eighth might, on its surface, pay homage to classicism, it is surely not a piece in the classical era style. It is pure Beethoven—quirky, original, and entirely modern.

E. Beethoven finished his Eighth Symphony in August 1812, although he was still fussing with its details as late as October. In November and December of 1812, Beethoven composed his tenth and last Sonata for Violin and Piano in G Major, Op. 96. The sonata opens with an exquisite, fluttering theme, shared equally by the violin and piano. (**Musical selection**: Sonata in G Major for Violin, Op. 96, movement 1 [1812].)

F. After he completed the Violin and Piano Sonata, Op. 96, Beethoven's mental health deteriorated and his creativity dissipated.

III. In the winter of 1812–1813, Beethoven was suffering both physically and mentally. In the spring of 1813, it had also become clear that his brother Casper Carl was in the last stages of tuberculosis, the same disease that had killed their mother.

    A. On May 27, 1813, Beethoven traveled to Baden, where he remained, except for a few weeks in July, until the middle of September. Friends in Baden were stunned by his physical and emotional condition.

    B. By the autumn of 1813, Beethoven's despair over the end of the Brentano affair brought him to the edge of a nervous breakdown.

        1. By the middle of 1813, he had fallen into such a state of mental and physical disorder that he could no longer compose, writing not a single work of significance during the year 1813.

        2. Beethoven was in mourning for his Immortal Beloved; some biographers suggest he was even suicidal.

    C. Sometime during the summer of 1813, Beethoven's friend, the inventor Johann Nepomuk Malzel, approached him with a proposition to compose a piece of music commemorating Wellington's defeat of Joseph Bonaparte's army in Spain.

        1. Malzel delivered what amounted to a "script concept." Beethoven turned the concept into a piece of orchestral music.

        2. Whatever the merits and flaws of the piece, Malzel and Beethoven chose the perfect moment to create a patriotic, anti-Napoleon piece of music.

        3. By late 1813, the Napoleonic tide had crested and was in serious retreat; after more than ten years of European warfare, Napoleon's end was in sight.

        4. During the summer of 1812, Napoleon marched on Russia with over 600,000 troops. He returned to Paris six months later, in December 1812, having abandoned what remained of his "Grand Army" to its fate.

5. On June 21, 1813, Lord Arthur Wellesley, Duke of Wellington, defeated a French army led by Napoleon's brother, the puppet "King of Spain" Joseph Bonaparte, at the Battle of Vittoria, in Northern Spain. The French army retreated back into France, abandoning Spain to the allies.

6. Four months later, on October 16–19, 1813, the defeat that finally broke the back of Napoleon and his empire took place at the Battle of Leipzig, also known as the Battle of Nations.

7. The news of Napoleon's rout and retreat from Leipzig hit the city of Vienna like a triple espresso. The Austrians, long accustomed to defeat and humiliation at the hands of the French, were beside themselves with patriotic fervor.

8. In December 1813, two concerts were given in Vienna for the benefit of Austrian and Bavarian soldiers who had been wounded in action. During these concerts, held on December 8 and 12, Beethoven's *Wellington's Victory* was first performed, to a level of acclaim that might be called hysterical.

9. All the leading musicians of Vienna participated in the performance, which according to Beethoven's biographer Alexander Thayer, "they viewed as a stupendous musical joke, and engaged in *con amore* as in a gigantic professional frolic."

10. Beethoven took the opportunity to premiere his Seventh Symphony alongside *Wellington's Victory*; the Seventh, much to Beethoven's dismay, came to be known as the "companion piece to *Wellington's Victory*."

D. As a result of the premieres of *Wellington's Victory* and the Seventh Symphony at these concerts, Beethoven suddenly attained a level of Viennese and Austrian popularity that he had never before experienced. Beethoven was so grateful that he wrote a public letter of thanks to everyone involved in the performances.

E. *Wellington's Victory*, Op. 91, is a loud bit of kitsch, in which the battle between the allies and the French is portrayed in series of obvious and tedious episodes.

1. In the opening of the movement, the approach of the two armies and the beginning of the battle is a veritable concerto for drums imitating guns.

2. From the right side of the orchestra, we hear, quietly at first, the approach of Wellington and his army in the music of *Rule, Britannia*.

3. The French army approaches from the left side of the orchestra, playing a then-popular French marching song, *Marlborough's March to War*.

4. Both armies in place, a series of "dueling fanfares" signals the advent of hostilities, which then break loose, featuring some of the most primitive and frankly simplistic music that Beethoven ever wrote. (**Musical selection**: *Wellington's Victory*, Op. 91, [1813].)

F. The Viennese loved this music in 1813 and 1814. For a period of time, *Wellington's Victory* was considered by the Viennese listening public to be Beethoven's single greatest work!

G. By the 1820s, *Wellington's Victory* had fallen out of the repertoire and was disparaged by critics.

IV. From a strictly monetary point of view, however, 1814 was the best year of Beethoven's life. Of the eleven public concerts held for Beethoven's benefit in his lifetime, five of them took place in 1814.

A. Beethoven's opera *Fidelio* was revived in 1814 to great success.

B. Beethoven's Symphony No. 8 in F Major, Op. 93, was premiered during this period on February 4, 1814. Also on the program were *Wellington's Victory* and Symphony No. 7 in A Major, Op. 92.

C. The seemingly universal acclaim of his music must have been incredibly gratifying for Beethoven, who had had been accused by his critics of being a "composer's composer," writing music of such complexity and aesthetic difficulty that it could be understood only by other composers and a few connoisseurs.

D. Less than a year before all these wonderful events, Beethoven had been languishing in Baden. He was still grieving for his Immortal Beloved, and as we've already noted, he wrote almost no music at all.

E. In 1814, Beethoven's newfound popularity and wealth stimulated his creativity. By early 1814, he was composing again and would continue to do so until the early months of 1815.

1. Unfortunately, the music he composed in 1814 was, like *Wellington's Victory*, meant to bank off the defeat of

Napoleon and to celebrate the victories of the allies and their royal leaders.

   2. Examples of this music include the operatic work *Germania*, WoO 94, written almost overnight to commemorate the surrender of Paris on March 31, 1814, and premiered at the Karntnertor-Theater on April 11, 1814; the choral *work Ihr weisen Grunder glucklicher Staaten* (*You Wise Founders of a Happy Nation*), WoO 95, written in honor of European leaders who gathered in Vienna in 1814 for the Congress of Vienna; *Der glorreiche Augenblick* (*The Glorious Moment*), Op. 136, a massive, full-blown cantata for four vocal soloists, full chorus, and orchestra and a fawning tribute to the Congress of Vienna, composed during the fall of 1814 and received with great acclaim.

F. As we close this lecture and anticipate Beethoven's fall from grace in 1815, let us sample a bit of his grand cantata *The Glorious Moment*, Op. 136, written in tribute to the assembled worthies of the Congress of Vienna.

   1. *The Glorious Moment*, often referred to as "The Congress Cantata," was premiered to the participants of the Congress of Vienna on November 29, 1814. Also on the program were the now familiar *Wellington's Victory* and Symphony No. 7.

   2. The obsequious text of the third movement goes so far as to praise such allies as Tsar Alexander I of Russia, King Friedrich Wilhelm III of Prussia, King Frederick VI of Denmark and Norway, King Maximilian I of Bavaria, and Emperor Franz I of Austria.

   3. These tributes are surprising coming from a composer who had, up to this point of his life, ferociously maintained his individuality and personal dignity in his dealings with the aristocracy. (**Musical selection**: *The Glorious Moment*, Op. 136, movement 1.)

Lecture Three
What Goes up Must Come down, 1815

Scope: Beethoven's return to fame and fortune was short lived. Six factors contributed to his fall from popular grace and his plunge into emotional instability. First, after *Wellington's Victory*, Beethoven believed that he had found the formula for success and composed a series of works that celebrated the victory of the allies over Napoleon. As soon as those events passed out of the moment, however, listeners realized that the music had no lasting artistic substance. Second, Beethoven showed no interest in exploring new musical styles and trends that were gaining popularity at the time. Third, in around 1815, Beethoven lost many of his most generous and loyal patrons. Also in 1815, Beethoven's hearing was deteriorating rapidly; he would be considered clinically deaf by 1818. During this same time, Viennese locals increasingly perceived Beethoven's career to be finished and the man himself, lunatic. Finally, Beethoven's treatment of his sister-in-law Johanna and his nephew Karl exposed many of his character flaws and delusions to the public eye.

Outline

I. As sudden as Beethoven's return to fame and fortune was in late 1813 and 1814, so was his fall from favor in 1815.

   A. Given our love for his music, we may find Beethoven's fall from popularity hard to understand, but we have had over 200 years to recognize his originality and to analyze the intricacies of his craft. In addition, we don't have to deal with Beethoven as a contemporary—he hasn't cheated us in his business dealings; we don't have to worry about being the object of his rage, or his often libelous comments, or the defendant in one of his lawsuits.

   B. There is nothing more temporary than the sort of excessive adulation Beethoven experienced in 1814 and early 1815. That adulation was not based on Beethoven's best music so much as it was a result of the excitement following Napoleon's defeat and the convening of the Congress of Vienna to create a "New Europe."

II. Beethoven's fall from popular grace—and his entrance into a dark emotional place from which he only slowly emerged four years later—can be attributed to six factors.

  A. Thrilled by the popular success of *Wellington's Victory*, Beethoven believed that he had found the musical formula for success and proceeded to compose a series of vocal, choral, and orchestral works that celebrated the allies who had defeated Napoleon (e.g., the grand cantata *The Glorious Moment*, Op. 136).

  1. This topical music of dubious artistic content was guaranteed to become irrelevant as soon as the historical circumstances that allowed for its creation waned from the communal consciousness.

  2. By late 1814 and early 1815, an increasing number of Beethoven's listening public recognized that these works had no lasting artistic substance.

  B. In post-Napoleonic Europe, new musical styles and trends were emerging, and Beethoven, at age forty-four, showed no desire to explore them.

  1. One such trend was the decorative, almost high-classical-revival styled music of Spohr, Moscheles, and Schubert—genuine musical "Biedermeier." (The term means "plain or ordinary Meyer," "Meyer" being the fictionalized last name of a working-class Joe. "Biedermeier style," then, is ordinary style, emphasizing simplicity, clean lines, and usefulness.) (**Musical selection**: Ludwig Spohr, Symphony No. 2 in D Minor, Op. 49, movement 4 [1820].)

  2. The new *Bel Canto* Italian musical style was personified by Gioacchino Rossini. Beethoven dismissed this style of music as being suitable only to "The frivolous and sensuous spirit of the times" (Scherman/Biancholli). (**Musical selection**: Rossini, *The Barber of Seville*, "Largo al Factotum" [1816].)

  3. Beethoven was also unwilling to deal with the sort of supernatural and gothic subjects that were increasingly popular in proto-Romantic German music, such as Carl Maria von Weber's opera *Der Freischutz* of 1821. Beethoven sarcastically remarked that such subjects have "A soporific effect on feeling and reason" (Scherman/Biancholli).

C. In and around the year 1815, one after another of Beethoven's most generous and loyal patrons were lost to him either as a result of death, permanent departure from Vienna, or personal estrangement.

1. Prince Ferdinand Kinsky died in late 1812.

2. Count Andreas Razumovsky (Op. 59, String Quartets Nos. 1–3) returned to Russia in 1815.

3. Prince Joseph Lobkowitz died in 1816.

4. Beethoven's most generous and influential patron, Prince Karl Lichnowsky, died in 1814.

5. Other of Beethoven's patrons turned, in 1815, to the new *Bel Canto* Italian opera while others, in the post-Napoleonic age, were impoverished.

D. In 1815, Beethoven's hearing was deteriorating rapidly, to the point that he would be considered clinically deaf by 1818.

1. In 1814 and 1815, Beethoven was still attempting to perform publicly as a pianist and conductor. This perseverance may demonstrate his extraordinary denial of his condition.

2. He suffered humiliation as a result of his own pig-headed insistence on performing.

3. For example, in April 1814, Beethoven participated in the premiere performance of his Trio No. 7 in Bb for Piano, Violin and 'Cello, Op. 97, the so-called "Archduke" trio. (**Musical selection**: Trio No. 7 in Bb ["Archduke"], Op. 97, movement 1 [1811].)

4. The composer and violinist Ludwig Spohr, who was present at the premiere, wrote that Beethoven's struggle with the music was pitiful.

5. Mercifully, Beethoven's last public performance as a pianist occurred nine months later, on January 25, 1815.

6. Unfortunately, Beethoven insisted on conducting the premiere of his Symphony No. 7 on December 8, 1813—the same concert that saw the triumph of *Wellington's Victory*.

7. Again, Ludwig Spohr wrote that Beethoven's deafness was evident in his conducting.

8. Spohr refers to a moment in the first movement of the Seventh Symphony during which the opening theme returns. Note the two *fermatas* (momentarily sustained notes), the second of which is very quiet—just the sort of thing that Beethoven would not hear. (**Musical selection**: Symphony No. 7 in A Major, Op. 92, movement 1, recapitulation [1812].)

E. Nine years later—long after his hearing was mostly gone—Beethoven was still attempting to conduct.

    1. In November 1822, he attempted to conduct the dress rehearsal of his opera *Fidelio*, which was being revived. The soprano Wilhelmine Schroder wrote that he obviously did not hear a single note and threw the singers and orchestra into confusion.

    2. Just eighteen months later, on May 7, 1824, Beethoven stood near the singers during the premiere of his Ninth Symphony and was unaware of the thunderous ovation it inspired until one of the singers gently turned him around to face the audience.

F. Beethoven was increasingly perceived as being washed up and insane.

    1. During these years, Beethoven never lost an opportunity to rail against the establishment—the courts, the aristocracy, even the emperor himself—forgetting entirely that he was living in a politically repressive police state.

    2. Beethoven seemed well aware that the locals thought he was crazy. In 1820, he wrote his friend Dr. Wilhelm Christian Muller: "Do not be misled by the Viennese, who regard me as crazy. If a sincere, independent opinion escapes me, as it often does, they think me mad" (Anderson).

G. The last and most important factor behind Beethoven's sustained emotional and professional decline beginning in 1815 had to do with his nephew Karl, the only child of his brother Casper and Casper's wife, Joanna. To understand the disastrous events surrounding Beethoven's relationship with Karl, we must look at his relationship with his brothers and his father, Johann van Beethoven.

III. Johann van Beethoven was an alcoholic. Certainly, the Beethoven family had a genetic predisposition toward alcoholism, and Johann's predisposition was reinforced by the circumstances of his life.

A. According to the psychoanalyst Edward Glover, "All the primary features of alcoholism represent fundamentally the individual's attempt to extricate himself from an impasse."

B. The impasse for Johann van Beethoven was his father, Ludwig, Sr.

    1. Apparently every aspect of Johann's life, including his education and career, was governed by his father's will.

    2. The absence of Johann's mother (committed, as she was, to the cloister) could only have intensified the father/son relationship.

    3. As we've previously observed, Ludwig, Sr., also lost no opportunity to tell anyone who would listen that his son would never amount to anything.

C. If Johann thought that marriage would relieve him of the burden of his father, he was wrong. He lacked the initiative and strength of spirit to make a life for himself and his family apart from his father.

    1. He never lived more than a couple of blocks from his father. The Fischers, who owned the house that the Beethovens lived in, recalled that Johann spent much of his time sitting at a window, staring out at the rain or making faces at his drinking companion, who lived across the street.

    2. Increasingly, Johann spent nights out with friends, crawling the taverns and wandering the streets, often not returning home until after sunrise.

D. Back at the house, Maria Magdalena van Beethoven played the role of the suffering and righteous wife of a worthless, footloose drunk. She complained constantly about her husband's drinking and debts, but she did not seem to have actively discouraged his drinking.

E. When Ludwig, Sr., died in December 1773, Johann van Beethoven inherited a not insignificant estate. One of his first acts was to pawn his recently deceased father's portrait.

F. Given his own emotional history and his growing dependence on alcohol, Johann van Beethoven was not a good candidate for fatherhood, but he became a father seven times over.

    1. The first child born to Johann and Maria Magdalena van Beethoven was a son named Ludwig Maria, who was baptized on April 2, 1769, and who died six days later.

    2. Their next child was Ludwig, baptized on December 17, 1770.

    3. Beethoven's two surviving brothers were born next: Casper Anton Carl, born in April 1774, was three-and-a-half years

Beethoven's junior, and Nikolaus Johann, born in October 1776, was nearly six years Beethoven's junior.

    4. Three more children were born to Johann and Maria Magdalena, but none of them survived their infancy.

G. On February 15, 1784, thirteen-year-old Ludwig van Beethoven petitioned the court for a formal appointment as assistant court organist. Along with the appointment, the young Beethoven asked for a raise, stating bluntly that his father was no longer capable of supporting his family.

H. Ludwig's musical instruction had begun at the age of four or five. That he was supremely gifted was quickly apparent. That Johann van Beethoven attempted to beat his son into becoming a musical prodigy was also apparent.

    1. Johann's treatment of Ludwig was brutal, and many anecdotes survive to corroborate his abuse.

    2. Johann succeeded in making his eldest son hate him passionately and, by extension, anyone else he perceived as an authority figure.

    3. Beethoven's mother did nothing in protest of her husband's treatment of her eldest son.

    4. Young Beethoven's response was to withdraw. He had few, if any, friends and did poorly at school.

    5. Music became, for Beethoven, a source of solace, strength, and even spirituality in the face of his domestic hardships.

I. Ludwig rejected his father completely, turning, instead, to his grandfather, Ludwig, Sr., for whom he maintained an almost unnatural reverence for the rest of his life.

    1. Ultimately, Beethoven's rejection of his father went far beyond merely embracing his grandfather as his essential male role model. Beethoven came to believe that Johann van Beethoven was not his biological father.

    2. Beethoven's fantasy regarding his paternity is something that Freud and his disciple Otto Rank dubbed the "Family Romance," in which an unhappy child replaces one or both parents with an "elevated" surrogate—a celebrity, a king, an athlete, even a fictional character.

    3. By 1790, Beethoven believed his birth date to be 1772, not 1770, as it really was. Beethoven claimed that the baptismal certificate with his name on it, dating from 1770, was actually that of his older brother, Ludwig Maria, who was born in 1769 and who died in infancy.

4. Beethoven increasingly believed himself to be the illegitimate son of the King of Prussia—either Frederick Wilhelm II (1744–1797) or his uncle, the great warrior-musician-king Frederick the Great (1712–1786).

5. Even near the end of his life, when he knew the fantasy to be untrue, Beethoven was still unwilling to publicly deny it.

Lecture Four
Beethoven and His Nephew, 1815–1819

Scope: Beethoven emerged from his shell during his second decade, through his musical talent and with the help of his teacher and mentor, Christian Gottlob Neefe. Neefe had been reared on the keyboard music of Johann Sebastian Bach and passed this influence on to his young student. By 1785, with Neefe's encouragement and tutelage, Beethoven had learned to play the organ and to conduct and had composed a number of works. After this promising start, Beethoven's responsibilities as the primary breadwinner and caregiver for his two younger brothers kept him from composing. In 1789, he petitioned the Elector to receive half of his father's pension and to have his father exiled from Bonn. When the Elector granted the petition, offering Beethoven some relief, he began a period of intense composition, the first of three "rebirths" during his lifetime.

The events of these years, however, would influence Beethoven's outrageous conduct in 1815 in the litigation over custody of his nephew Karl. Beethoven became irrationally possessive and jealous of his brothers in his youth. When his brother Carl died later in life, Beethoven transferred these feelings to his nephew and pursued four years of destructive litigation to gain guardianship of the boy. During these years, Beethoven's deepest fears and longings were brought to the surface and some of his most long-held delusions were destroyed. The events would also serve as a catalyst for Beethoven's next "rebirth," in 1819, and the creation of the Ninth Symphony, the *Missa Solemnis*, the last piano sonatas, and the six late string quartets

Outline

I. Beethoven emerged from his shell, via his musical talent, during his second decade. In 1782, at the age of eleven, he was appointed assistant court organist at the Electoral Court.

A. Although it was an unsalaried position, it lifted Beethoven out of the environment of his house and into that of the court. It boosted his self-esteem as both a person and as a musician.

B. In June 1784, at the age of thirteen-and-a-half, Beethoven was appointed deputy court organist. This was an official and professional appointment, which carried with it a salary of 150 florins and gave Beethoven the feeling that he was now the equal to his father in music.

C. Beethoven had, in fact, far outstripped his father as a musician, which even Johann realized.

D. Young Beethoven began working with Christian Gottlob Neefe (1748–1798), who became more than a music instructor to Ludwig; he became Beethoven's friend and mentor and the person responsible for Beethoven's explosive development as a performing musician and composer in the 1780s.

II. Neefe was born in Chemnitz, a north-central German city southeast of Leipzig.

A. Trained as a composer, organist, and conductor, he settled in Bonn in 1779 and was appointed principal court organist on February 15, 1781. By that time, he had probably already been entrusted with Beethoven's musical education.

B. Neefe remained Beethoven's primary teacher for twelve years, until Beethoven left Bonn forever in 1792.

C. Note that Neefe was Lutheran and had been reared on the keyboard music of Johann Sebastian Bach, who had lived his last twenty-seven years in Leipzig. Neefe was two years old and living just a few miles away in Chemnitz when Bach died in Leipzig in 1750.

D. By the time Beethoven began working with Neefe, in 1780 or 1781, Bach's music had fallen on hard times.

    1. Considered unnecessarily complex, elitist, and expressively overblown, Bach's music, like most music of the high Baroque, had been rejected by the aesthetes and pedants of the classical era.

    2. Neefe was an exception to this anti-Bach rule. The keyboard music of Bach played an overwhelming role in Neefe's education of the young Beethoven.

      3. The infinite spirituality and depth of feeling, absolute precision and compactness of means, and extraordinary craft of Bach's music were indelibly printed in Beethoven's hands and mind.

      4. No composer of his generation was more profoundly influenced by the music of Bach than Beethoven.

      5. That influence became more and more apparent as Beethoven grew older. By the end of his life, Beethoven's music aimed for an expressive depth and polyphonic clarity that was more closely related to Bach than to classicism.

E. To Neefe's eternal credit, he quickly recognized Beethoven's genius and was unstinting in his praise and encouragement of the boy.

      1. Neefe quickly taught Beethoven to play the organ and to conduct the court orchestra.

      2. Neefe also arranged to have some of Beethoven's early compositions published and even wrote an article about Beethoven, which appeared in Cramer's *Magazin der Musik*.

      3. In the following early composition, note the simple, march-like theme; the straightforward arrangement; and the somewhat pedestrian series of nine variations. (**Musical selection at piano**: Nine Variations in C Minor on a March by Dressler, WoO 63, theme [1782].)

F. By 1785, Beethoven had composed a number of works, including the Three Piano Sonatas, WoO 47 (1782–1783); a Piano Concerto in Eb Major, WoO 4 (1784); and Three Quartets for Piano and Strings, WoO 36 (1785). Beethoven also made rapid progress as a pianist and organist; by 1785, he was clearly a budding virtuoso.

G. At age thirteen or fourteen, the young Beethoven, who had been abused and withdrawn a few years before, must have felt enormously liberated and empowered to play the music of Bach on the huge Electoral Court organ. (**Musical selection**: Johann Sebastian Bach, *Fantasia and Fugue in G Minor* ["The Great"], BWV 542 [ca. 1715].)

III. After the promising start made between 1781 and 1785, Beethoven does not seem to have composed anything between 1785 and 1789.

A. Life was not pleasant at the Beethoven house. By the mid-1780s, Beethoven's father had become a hopeless alcoholic.

B. By 1785, Ludwig had become the sole breadwinner for his family. By 1788, his professional responsibilities included playing the organ at court, playing the viola in the court and theater orchestras, teaching music, and performing as a solo pianist. Given his responsibilities at home and at court, he had little time for composing.

C. In the spring of 1787, the authorities in Bonn decided to send their young genius to Vienna so that the Viennese authorities could evaluate his future worth as a pianist; perhaps he might even play for, and take lessons from, Mozart.

D. Less then two weeks into his stay, Beethoven received word that his mother had become quite ill (her tuberculosis had entered its terminal phase). Beethoven hurried back home.

E. Maria Magdalena van Beethoven died on July 17, 1787. Beethoven did not return to Vienna after her death. The Elector later complained in a letter to Haydn that Beethoven's trip to Vienna was a complete failure, with Beethoven bringing home "nothing but debts."

F. Ludwig van Beethoven, sixteen-and-a-half years old, became the head of the household and the primary caregiver to his two younger brothers. He had to deal with the family finances and the consequences of his father's drunkenness.

G. Ultimately, the responsibility was too much for Beethoven to handle. In late 1789, he petitioned the Elector, requesting that half of his father's pension be paid directly to himself and his brothers and that his father be exiled from Bonn.

H. Coinciding precisely with the petition to the Elector, late 1789 marked a breakthrough for Beethoven, a period of intense composition that continued until his departure for Vienna in November 1792.
   1. The music he wrote during this period includes five sets of piano variations, ballet music, concert arias, songs, chamber works for piano and winds, a piano trio, and two full-blown cantatas for vocal soloists, chorus, and orchestra.

2. The extraordinary *Funeral Cantata on the Death of Emperor Joseph II* for solo voices, chorus, and orchestra dates from 1790. We'll listen to the orchestral introduction and the subsequent opening number chorus for chorus and vocal soloists. (**Musical selection**: *Funeral Cantata on the Death of Emperor Joseph II*, No. 1 [1790].)

3. Beethoven had come of age in 1789, as a man and as a musician, and the result was a rebirth of self, the first of what would be three such "rebirths" in his life: 1789, 1803, and 1819.

4. This last "rebirth," of 1819, came about only after the excruciating events of 1815–1819, events that began with Beethoven's fall from popularity in 1815 and moved through the horrific litigation over the custody of his nephew Karl.

IV. As an adult, Beethoven was conflicted in his feelings toward his brothers, for whom he had become surrogate mother and father when he was but sixteen-and-a-half years old.

A. On one hand, Beethoven remained irrationally possessive toward his brothers and, conversely, implacably hostile toward their wives, Johanna (Casper's wife) and Therese (Johann's wife).

B. On the other hand, he was terribly jealous of both his brothers, who managed to have sustained relationships with women. At times, Beethoven's behavior towards his brothers was intrusive and ridiculous.

C. Ultimately, the conflicted feeling and irrational possessiveness Beethoven felt toward his brothers was transferred to his nephew Karl after his brother Casper died in November 1815.

1. Casper Carl van Beethoven and Johanna Reiss were married on May 25, 1806. A little over three months later, in September, Johanna gave birth to their only child, Karl.

2. Beethoven opposed his brother's marriage from the start and reacted prudishly at the birth of the child.

3. On November 14, 1815, the dying Casper added a codicil to his will explicitly stating that he wanted custody of his son to remain with Johanna, not Beethoven.

4. The day after adding this codicil to his will, Casper died. In direct contravention to Casper's dying wish, Beethoven immediately claimed to be Karl's one and only guardian.

5. Within a month, Beethoven had petitioned the Imperial and Royal *Landrecht* of Lower Austria, as well as the civil court (*Magistrat der Stadt Wien*), for sole possession of Karl; five weeks after Casper died, Beethoven petitioned the *Landrecht* of Lower Austria for a second time.

6. It's a sad testament to Beethoven's fame and his influential friends that on January 9, 1816, the *Landsrecht* ruled in Beethoven's favor, appointing him Karl's only legal guardian.

7. On February 2, 1816, a weeping Karl, nine years old, was forcibly taken from his hysterical mother and placed, against his will, in Cajetan Giannattasio Del Rio's private school for boys.

D. Beethoven's action were appalling and, unfortunately, only the beginning. Johanna did not intend to give up her son without a fight, which ultimately went on for four years and came close to destroying the lives of everyone involved.

E. Johanna van Beethoven was, by all neutral accounts, a decent and intelligent woman. Beethoven's mistreatment of her remains one of the ugliest and most sordid affairs in his life.

F. The consensus of psychological scholars is that Beethoven truly believed that he was rescuing Karl from an unfit mother. Almost from the beginning, however, issues that went far beyond mere custody of Karl seemed to be driving Beethoven's actions. A number of delusions emerged that suggest that Beethoven was beginning to have trouble distinguishing fantasy from reality.

1. Beethoven began to suspect—without any basis in reality—that Johanna had killed Casper with poison. Not until Beethoven had received the personal assurances of the attending physician did he let go of this fantasy.

2. Beethoven soon began to believe that Johanna was having him followed for unscrupulous reasons; in February 1816, he claimed that she had bribed his servant for some unstated purpose unrelated to her son.

3. Later in February 1816, he began to suspect that Johanna was a prostitute.

G. By 1816, Beethoven had come to regard his "rescue" of Karl as a heroic, divinely authorized mission. Certainly by 1816, Beethoven the composer had exhausted his symbolic exploration of heroism;

the single, childless, almost-deaf, forty-six-year-old Beethoven was now creating and enacting a bizarre "heroic" drama in an attempt to conquer his deepest fears and existential loneliness.

H. Beethoven's central delusion in this pathological sequence of events grew until he actually began to convince himself that he had become a father in reality.

    1. It has also been suggested that Beethoven's fantasy—that he was the real physical father of Karl—implies that he imagined himself to have had relations with Johanna.

    2. It's not difficult to interpret Beethoven's terrible treatment of Johanna as an attempt to ward off his own desire for her.

    3. These interpretations are speculation, of course, but Beethoven's actions toward Johanna cannot be explained by anything that Johanna actually said or did to him in reality. According to Freud, the more powerful the feeling of love, the greater the opposite feeling necessary to hold it in check.

I. The contradictions and conflicts Beethoven felt for Johanna were only outdone by those he felt for Karl. At one moment, Beethoven could be a loving and caring "uncle" and the next, a neglectful, inconsiderate, sometimes even violent disciplinarian.

J. Johanna was distraught. We read that she would disguise herself as a man and come to the school playground so that she could watch Karl during recess.

K. In 1818, she went back to the *Landrecht*, the aristocratic legal body over which Beethoven's rich friends had influence. All her petitions were initially denied.

L. On December 3, 1818, Karl, now twelve years old, ran away from school and went to his mother. The police again came and took him away, but Johanna, fortified by this sign of Karl's love and stunned by revelations of Beethoven's mistreatment of the boy, went back to court again, this time with a first-rate attorney.

M. Ultimately, it wasn't the damning testimony that caused the *Landrecht* to dismiss the case from its jurisdiction and remand it to a civil court (where Johanna would have a fighting chance to get her son back); it was the revelation that Beethoven was not, as he had claimed for so long, of "noble" birth.

1. These legal proceedings proved without doubt that Ludwig van Beethoven had been born in 1770 and was the son of the alcoholic Johann van Beethoven, not the royal bastard of Frederick the Great.

2. The idea that he was of common birth and that his court case should be heard in civil court rankled Beethoven to the core of his being.

3. The civil courts had no patience for Beethoven or with his legal position in the litigation. Beethoven's other brother, Nikolaus Johann, joined Johanna in attempting to protect Karl from Beethoven.

4. On September 17, 1819, the *Magistrat* of the civil court awarded guardianship of Karl to his mother. Beethoven's appeals were denied, but the litigation did not end.

5. Both Archduke Rudolf Johann Joseph Rainer and Archduke Ludwig—members of the imperial family—interceded with the court of appeals on Beethoven's behalf.

6. On April 8, 1820, the court of appeals reversed its earlier decision and found for Beethoven, making him again Karl's sole guardian.

7. Johanna appealed the decision to the emperor but to no avail. On July 24, 1820, the courts ruled the case closed.

N. Johanna, exhausted and undoubtedly wanting to replace the child that Beethoven stole from her, got pregnant and remarried. In doing so, she forfeited forever her rights to Karl. She gave birth to a daughter, whom she named Ludovica, the feminine form of "Ludwig."

V. When Beethoven began composing again around 1820, he had once again reinvented himself, writing music the likes of which no one had ever even imagined before.

A. We can only speculate as to what degree the fight over Karl was responsible for shaping Beethoven's late compositional language.

B. The years 1815–1820 saw Beethoven's deepest fears and longings brought to the surface; his pretense to noble birth was destroyed, as was his "Family Romance" and his long-held conviction that he was a royal bastard.

C. Certainly, Karl and Johanna had served as catalysts for Beethoven's next incarnation of his artistic self, one that would see the creation of the Ninth Symphony, the *Missa Solemnis*, the last piano sonatas, and the six late string quartets.

Lecture Five
Beethoven the Pianist

Scope: Aside from the Piano Sonata in Bb, Op. 106, called the
Hammerklavier Sonata, Beethoven wrote little significant music in
the period 1815–1819. The *Hammerklavier* is a majestic piece of
music, and its completion, in 1818, corresponds with Beethoven's
third reinvention of himself as a composer. By 1820, Beethoven
was well into his third compositional period, which encompassed
such masterworks as the Great Mass, the *Missa Solemnis*, Op. 123,
and the Symphony No. 9 in D Minor, Op. 125. Before this period,
in 1792, Beethoven was living in Vienna with a reputation as a
virtuoso pianist in a city that was mad for pianists. He outplayed
virtually every other pianist in the city in competitions and became
the darling of the Viennese aristocracy. During this same time, he
took lessons with Haydn, although his dislike of authority figures
made most music lessons a waste of time.

Outline

I. Although Beethoven wrote little music of consequence between 1815–
1819, he was not musically inactive.

   A. The popularity of Beethoven's music, particularly outside Vienna,
   was skyrocketing, surpassing even that of Haydn and Mozart;
   however, he wrote little significant music between 1815–1819.

   B. The Piano Sonata in Bb, Op. 106, nicknamed the *Hammerklavier*,
   stands out as one of the few masterworks begun and completed
   during these years, having been composed between 1817–1818.
      1. Beethoven considered the *Hammerklavier* Sonata to be his
      best piano music to date. It is also the longest of his piano
      sonatas; in fact, of Beethoven's symphonies, only the Third
      and the Ninth are longer than the *Hammerklavier*.
      2. Powerful and revolutionary though the *Hammerklavier* Sonata
      is, it is also, in some ways, a "back-to-basics" work for
      Beethoven.
      3. The year Beethoven finished the piece, 1818, and his
      reinvention of himself as a composer correspond with the final
      disintegration of his hearing, his coming to grips with the

Immortal Beloved affair, and the deep-seated conflicts, desires, and delusions that were forced to the surface as a result of the fight over Karl.

C. Like the Third Symphony, Op. 55, and the *Appassionata* Piano Sonata, Op. 57—two "breakthrough" works of Beethoven's second self-reinvention (1803–1805)—the *Hammerklavier* Sonata is a majestic, heroic, and magnificent piece of music, written with little regard for the physical limits of the piano as it existed around 1818.

  1. Beethoven may have been inspired to write this sonata as a result of the gift of a piano from an English company. This piano would have been capable of much more volume and resonance than the lighter, Viennese pianos Beethoven was familiar with. Let's hear the magnificent, orchestral opening of the first movement played on a period instrument. (**Musical selection**: Piano Sonata in Bb Major, Op. 106, *Hammerklavier*, movement 1, opening.)

  2. Given the dramatic scope and breadth of this music, it sounds weak on the period piano. The music demands a level sonority and dynamic contrast that was simply unavailable on the pianos of Beethoven's time. Listen to it played on a modern piano. (**Musical selection**: Piano Sonata in Bb Major, Op. 106, *Hammerklavier*, movement 1, opening.)

  3. Some of the original instrument recordings available of Beethoven's symphonies are nothing short of a revelation in terms of their precision and balance. But with Beethoven's late piano music, we see that he was looking past the pianos of his time, toward an instrument capable of orchestral power and organ-like resonance.

  4. The second movement of the *Hammerklavier* is a crackling *scherzo*. (**Musical selection** [modern piano]: Piano Sonata in Bb Major, Op. 106, *Hammerklavier*, movement 2, opening.)

  5. The third movement of the *Hammerklavier* constitutes the spiritual core of the sonata. This unique music reminds us that underneath Beethoven's unhappiness and misanthropy was tenderness, sensitivity, and humanity. (**Musical selection** [modern piano]: Piano Sonata in Bb Major, Op. 106, *Hammerklavier*, movement 3, opening.)

6. The fourth and last movement of the *Hammerklavier* is a fugue, preceded by a slow introduction. Beethoven rightly decided that to start the fugue immediately after the long and sublime third movement would cause a musical disruption. Beethoven also instructs us that the fugue should be performed, "*con alcune licenze*," "with some license" or "freely." (**Musical selection** [modern piano]: Piano Sonata in Bb Major, Op. 106, *Hammerklavier*, movement 4, fugue opening.)

II. By 1820, Beethoven's compositional rebirth was well on its way and, with it, his so-called third, or late, compositional period.

    A. In 1820, he completed the Piano Sonata in E Major, Op. 109.

    B. In 1821, he completed the Piano Sonata in Ab Major, Op. 110.

    C. In 1822, Beethoven completed:

        1. Piano Sonata in C Minor, Op. 111 (the last of his thirty-two piano sonatas);

        2. The Great Mass, the *Missa Solemnis*, Op. 123;

        3. The *Overture to the Consecration of the House*, Op. 124;

        4. The *Diabelli Variations* for Piano, Op. 120;

    D. In 1824, Beethoven completed the Symphony No. 9 in D Minor, Op. 125.

    E. From the spring of 1824 through December of 1826, Beethoven composed his last five string quartets (Op. 127, 130, 131, 132, and 135) and the *Grosse Fugue* for String Quartet, Op. 133.

    F. Biographer Maynard Solomon describes Beethoven at this time: "Everything was subordinated to his work…He had reached a stage where he had become wholly possessed by his art."

    G. In the 1820s, Beethoven was in many ways a man apart from the every day world. Before we examine these last years, however, we must return to 1792, three years after the beginning of Beethoven's great compositional rebirth of 1789.

III. In November 1792, Beethoven was almost twenty-two years old and his life was relatively pleasant. He was in the process of moving to Vienna to study with Joseph Haydn, the master of Austrian/German music.

A. By 1792, Beethoven had achieved a growing, if local, reputation as a virtuoso pianist and composer of great promise.

    1. When Haydn passed through Bonn during the late spring of 1792, he had had the opportunity to meet the local talent. He was particularly taken with the music of young Beethoven who, on the request of the Elector, Haydn accepted as a student.

    2. Beethoven had many good friends, as evidenced by the fifteen entries in his "farewell" autograph album, entries that date from between October 24 to November 1, 1792.

    3. Perhaps the most intriguing of these entries is the one from Beethoven's first great patron, Count Ferdinand Waldstein. Waldstein predicted that Beethoven's trip to Vienna would be "the fulfillment of your long-frustrated wishes." Beethoven would later dedicate his Piano Sonata in C Major, Op. 53, the so-called "Waldstein" Sonata to his patron. (**Musical selection**: Piano Sonata in C Major, Op. 53, "Waldstein," movement 1, opening [1804].)

B. Beethoven left Bonn on November 3 or 4, 1792.

    1. Though Beethoven had every intention of returning to Bonn, circumstances—and feelings—would change. As it turned out, he never set foot in Bonn again, not even to visit the graves of his mother and father.

    2. Even as Beethoven was preparing to leave Bonn, Johann van Beethoven was dying of heart disease. On December 18, 1792, roughly six weeks after Beethoven arrived in Vienna and had begun what amounted to a new life, Johann van Beethoven died.

IV. When Beethoven arrived in Vienna in late 1792, he was initially known as a virtuoso pianist; as a composer, he was considered still a student.

A. The Viennese were mad for pianists during the late 18th century. According to Arthur Loesser, as many as 6,000 piano students and more than 300 professional pianists lived in Vienna at this time.

B. As a pianist, Beethoven was essentially self-taught; he had certainly received more training as an organist than as a piano player. Indeed, by 1792, he exhibited an extraordinary but unconventional technique and an original approach to the still new "pianoforte."

C. The Viennese had never heard anybody play the piano like Beethoven. Accustomed to the fluent harpsichord-derived technique of Mozart and Clementi, the Viennese found Beethoven's playing something of a revelation and a disaster for the lightweight pianos themselves. Beethoven, hands held high, smashed every piano he touched, aiming always for more volume, more resonance, more expressive power.

D. At one time or another, Beethoven outplayed every pianist in Vienna in competitions.

E. Beethoven also became the darling of the Austro-Hungarian aristocracy, whose members vied with one another to have him in their homes and lavish him with gifts and money; their status rose and fell as he would bestow, or not bestow, his favor on potential patrons.

    1. Beethoven's appearance was somewhat strange. He was short, with a thick body, and an unusually large head, covered, of course, with his long, wild hair.

    2. Beethoven was also physically clumsy; he was liable to knock over or break anything he touched. He was uncoordinated, never learned to dance, and had problems cutting and shaping quill pens for himself.

    3. In addition, Beethoven was a slob. His flat was described by the Baron de Tremont as "the darkest, most disorderly place imaginable."

    4. In short, Beethoven was haughty, sloppy, unafraid, self-centered, supremely individualistic, independent, and disrespectful.

V. Never was Beethoven's abject inability to deal respectfully with authority more apparent than in his lessons with Haydn, which were a waste of time for both men.

A. At twenty-two, Beethoven had a persecution complex and a pathologic dislike of anything or anyone he perceived as an "authority figure."

B. The sixty-year-old Josef Haydn, recently returned from London, was a disinterested teacher at best and was also grieving over the recent deaths of his two best friends, Wolfgang Mozart and Marianne Genzinger.

C. Beethoven began his "lessons" with Haydn almost immediately after his arrival in Vienna in November 1792.

1. It soon became apparent—at least to Beethoven—that Haydn was neither a systematic nor a conscientious teacher and that his counterpoint exercises were not being properly marked.

2. Beethoven secretly hired another teacher, Johann Schenk (1761–1830), to correct the assignments, which Beethoven then copied out anew to make it appear as if he had done everything right the first time.

3. Haydn discovered the subterfuge after a year, in December 1793, but his disenchantment with Beethoven was a result of something more distressing than the lessons with Schenk.

4. On November 23, 1793, still unaware that Beethoven was anything other than an honest and devoted student, Haydn wrote a letter to Elector Maximilian Franz in Bonn, expressing both his pride in Beethoven's "progress" and his concern over Beethoven's financial situation.

5. The Elector replied that the bulk of the music Beethoven purported to have composed in Vienna had actually been written and performed in Bonn before he left. In addition, the Elector informed Haydn that Beethoven's allotment was 900 florins, significantly more than Haydn seemed to think it was.

6. Haydn was mortified; Beethoven had borrowed money from him, lied to him about his income, and deceived him about when he had written the music that Haydn had sent to the Elector.

D. The lessons with Haydn abruptly ended, although Beethoven did, eventually, obtain Haydn's pardon.

E. Beethoven did not return to Bonn and went on to study with Johann Albrechtsberger and Antonio Salieri with limited success. According to Beethoven's friend and student Ferdinand Ries, his teachers said, "that Beethoven was always so stubborn and self-willed that he had to learn from his own bitter experience what he had never been willing to accept in the course of his lessons."

Lecture Six
Beethoven the Composer, 1792–1802

Scope: The period between 1792–1802 is generally referred to as Beethoven's "Viennese" period, a time of assimilation, technical growth, and mastery of the existing Viennese classical style. The year 1795 was the first significant year of Beethoven's compositional career, which saw the publication of the Opus 1 Trios for Piano, Violin, and 'Cello and the premiere of the Piano Concerto No. 2. These works already exhibit originality, drama, and scale that are outside the classical tradition, as did Beethoven's early piano sonatas. For a period of eighteen months, Beethoven next devoted himself to the genre of the string quartet, eventually composing six, published as Opus 18, Nos. 1–6. These quartets marked a significant advancement in Beethoven's career as a composer. Next, Beethoven turned to the symphony, premiering his Symphony No. 1 in C Major in 1800. On the surface a conservative piece, this symphony is also full of witticisms, shocking harmonic events, and unique organic developments.

In 1801, Beethoven's career and finances were flourishing, but he was in poor health. His hearing loss, which had begun in 1796, was becoming progressively worse, and Beethoven's despair over it came to a head in 1802. In that year, he wrote what is known as the Heiligenstadt Testament, a letter to his brothers that is part confessional, part apology, and part last will and testament. Writing the letter may well have been a catharsis for Beethoven, spurring yet another reinvention of himself in the guise of a hero.

Outline

I. Although Beethoven's counterpoint lessons with Haydn were unproductive, his personal and private study of the works of Haydn himself, along with Bach and Mozart, were irreplaceable. Beethoven's study of this music formed his essential compositional education.

   A. Slowly but steadily, Beethoven's reputation as a pianist was joined by his reputation as a composer, although we should note that Beethoven avoided writing symphonies or string quartets until he was prepared, emotionally and professionally, to be compared to Haydn and Mozart.

B. Compositionally, we generally refer to the period between 1792–1802 as Beethoven's "Viennese" period, a period of technical growth and mastery of the *pre-existing* Viennese classical style.

C. We must remember, however, that even as Beethoven was mastering his technique, his compositional voice was always unique. From the beginning, his early music exhibited a power and depth of expression that, despite its "classical" surface, mark it as Beethoven's own. We will consider, for example, his three Trios for Piano, Violin, and 'Cello, published as Opus 1, Nos. 1, 2, and 3, in 1795.

II. The year 1795, when Beethoven was twenty-four, was the first significant year in his compositional career.

A. The great events of 1795 were the publication of the Opus 1 Trios for Piano, Violin, and 'Cello and the premiere of the Piano Concerto in Bb (a piece we now know as Piano Concerto No. 2, even though it was written long before the work known as Piano Concerto No. 1, Op. 15).

B. Beethoven's Piano Concerto No. 2 was begun back in Bonn, as early as 1785 and certainly no later than 1790.

    1. He rewrote the piece twice after arriving in Vienna; the second of these rewritten versions is the one we are familiar with today. Let's sample the bracing and engaging third movement. (**Musical selection**: Piano Concerto No. 2 in Bb, movement 3 [1798].)

    2. On the surface, the music is charming and direct, fully within the classical style. If we had time for a detailed look at this last movement, however, we would discover rhythmic and harmonic elements that lie outside the classical tradition.

C. No such detailed look is necessary to see how Beethoven's Piano Trios Op. 1 lie outside the classical tradition; their originality is right on the surface.

    1. Up to the time Beethoven wrote these works, the piano trio was considered a vehicle for amateur performers. Mozart's and Haydn's trios, for example, are short works that make limited demands on the performers.

2. Like his early piano sonatas, however, Beethoven's Trios Op. 1 are big, almost symphonic works. Each is four movements long, each requires a considerable degree of virtuosity to perform, and each one runs about twenty-five to thirty minutes.

3. For Beethoven's contemporaries, hearing these trios for the first time is like watching Olympic badminton for the first time. We might be thrilled by the athleticism of the players but taken aback by the fact that such a familiar backyard pastime could become an activity for virtuosos.

D. When the trios were performed for the first time, Haydn advised Beethoven not to publish the third Trio in C Minor. Haydn's remark, of course, led Beethoven to believe that he was jealous.

1. In reality, Haydn simply didn't understand the function of a long, dramatic, minor-mode piano trio. In Haydn's mind, a piano trio was a vehicle for amateurs; big, dramatic musical ideas belonged in a string quartet or a symphony. (**Musical selection**: Piano Trio in E Flat Major, Op. 1, No. 1, movement 1, exposition: both dramatic and lyric themes [1795].)

2. To us, this sounds like music of the classical era. For the musicians of the time, however, this music was wild, exciting, and controversial, music that sounded uniquely like Beethoven.

III. Beethoven's early piano sonatas are, likewise, conceived on a grand scale.

A. For example, the first movement of the Piano Sonata No. 8 in C Minor, the so-called "*Pathetique*," of 1797, begins with a huge, sonorous, genuinely symphonic introduction. (**Musical selection at piano**: Piano Sonata No. 8 in C Minor, Op. 13, movement 1, introduction [1797].)

B. The lyric theme of the second movement remains one of the most popular and familiar melodies Beethoven ever wrote. (**Musical selection at piano**: Piano Sonata No. 8 in C Minor, Op. 13, movement 2 [1797].)

C. The third movement is a bristling and dramatic rondo based on the following theme. (**Musical selection**: Piano Sonata No. 8 in C Minor, Op. 13, movement 3, rondo theme.)

IV. For a period of eighteen consecutive months, in 1798 and 1799, Beethoven dedicated himself entirely to the genre of the string quartet, eventually composing six string quartets, published as Opus 18, Nos. 1–6.

   A. By writing these six string quartets, Beethoven brought himself into direct comparison (or competition?) with Mozart and Haydn. Beethoven believed that he was both technically and emotionally up to the comparison, and he was right.

   B. The six string quartets Op. 18 were, for Beethoven, his artistic "coming out."

      1. The string quartet in 1798 was the preeminent chamber combination for both professional and amateur performers; the singular rigor of writing for four string voices—soprano, alto, tenor, and bass—was and remains one of the great artistic challenges any composer can take on.

      2. Beethoven's Op. 18 string quartets were significant for Beethoven both artistically and in terms of his career advancement as a composer.

   C. We will take a brief look at two of the six Op. 18 quartets—the first one to be composed and the last one to be composed.

      1. Beethoven's String Quartet in D Major, Op. 18, No. 3, despite its designation as "No. 3," is the first of the Op. 18 quartets he composed.

      2. Despite its many marvelous and fresh ideas, its harmonic ingenuity and distinctive contrapuntal devices, this first quartet does not stray from the model of the four-movement classical-era string quartet established by Joseph Haydn.

      3. The first movement of Beethoven's first string quartet is an elegant, refined movement of graceful themes and muted contrasts. (**Musical selection**: String Quartet in D Major, Op. 18, No. 3, movement 1 [1798].)

      4. The second movement is lyric and decorative, no more and no less. (**Musical selection**: String Quartet in D Major, Op. 18, No. 3, movement 2.)

      5. The third movement is, according to Joseph Kerman, "A spotlessly groomed little piece whose one interest seems to be in making itself inconspicuous." (**Musical selection**: String Quartet in D Major, Op. 18, No. 3, movement 3.)

6. The fourth movement, as we would expect based on the "model," is frisky, ingenious, and upbeat. (**Musical selection**: String Quartet in D Major, Op. 18, No. 3, movement 4.)

7. Of Beethoven's first string quartet and this four-movement model, Joseph Kerman writes, "In this, his first string quartet, Beethoven had not found a way out of the Classical scheme of essentially independent movements within the four-movement framework. It is not even certain that he fully appreciated the need to get out [of that preexisting scheme]."

8. We now jump forward to the last three quartets of Op. 18— Nos. 4, 5, and 6—which were written in chronological order. By these later quartets, Beethoven does indeed appreciate the "need" to break with the model.

9. The most striking act of large-scale originality of all the Op. 18 string quartets occurs in No. 6 in Bb Major, the last to be composed. That act of striking originality is the insertion of a fifth movement into the traditional four-movement scheme.

10. Beethoven's "extra" movement is a pained, deeply personal *adagio* stuck in between the third movement *scherzo* and the frisky and upbeat final movement. Beethoven labeled this "extra" movement "*La Malinconia*," "The Melancholic," and added in the score: "This piece is to be played with the greatest delicacy."

11. The movement displays a harmonic instability and fragmented melodic surface that are striking even to our jaded ears today. Truly, "The Melancholic" is a musical "lost soul." (**Musical selection**: String Quartet in Bb Major, Op. 18, No. 6, *La Malinconia*, ms. 1–21 [1799].)

12. The mere existence of such an "extra" movement, inserted into the four-movement model, came as a shock to its contemporary audience. Its intensely personal message; the dark, expressive pall it casts over the entire quartet; and the way in which this melancholy music returns during the fifth and final movement of the quartet is unique to Beethoven.

V. Armed with the success of his Opus 18 string quartets, Beethoven decided to tackle that most prestigious genre of instrumental music, the symphony.

A. On April 2, 1800, Beethoven staged the first public concert of his works, a so-called "*Akademie*," during which he premiered his Symphony No. 1 in C Major, completed just weeks before.

B. The symphony is a decidedly conservative work; again, Beethoven knew the piece would be judged against the symphonies of Haydn and Mozart.

    1. In addition, Beethoven, aware of the fact that this was his first major public concert, wanted to make a good impression on the general listening public.

    2. In this, Beethoven succeeded all too well. To his eternal annoyance, his First Symphony remained the most popular of his symphonies with the general public through his entire life!

C. Beethoven's First is also full of witticisms, shocking harmonic events, orchestrational details, and unique organic developments.

    1. For example, the first movement of Beethoven's First Symphony begins with the slow, solemn introduction we associate with many of Haydn's symphonies. (**Musical selection**: Symphony No. 1 in C Major, Op. 21, movement 1, introduction, opening.)

    2. On the surface, Beethoven's introduction at the beginning of his first symphony would seem to be a tip of his musical hat to Haydn and the classical tradition, but Beethoven's introduction is also much more.

    3. If we listen to the first four measures of the introduction, we hear a series of dominant—dissonant—harmonies resolving upward, not a single one of them to the home key of C Major. Instead, we hear a chromatic ascent to an A. The result is tonal ambiguity. (**Musical selection at piano**: Opening four measures of introduction.)

    4. In the context of its time, given the language of its day, this introduction was shocking.

    5. Keep in mind that Beethoven never does anything for dramatic or shock value alone; there are always sound and organic reasons behind his compositional decisions.

    6. In due time, we arrive in C Major and a lively, straightforward theme emerges in the strings. (**Musical selection**: Symphony No. 1 in C Major, Op. 21, movement 1, theme 1.)

7. Now listen to the harmonies that underlie this peppy little theme. (**Musical selection at piano**: Harmonic underpinning of theme 1.)

8. All these repeated harmonies reduce to the following progression. (**Musical selection at piano**: Reduction.)

9. Compare the reduction to the rising dissonances of the introduction. (**Musical selection at piano**: Introduction, ms. 1–4.)

10. The introduction is, in reality, the harmonic underpinning of theme 1. Beethoven took the harmonic underpinning of the opening theme and in the introduction, placed it on the musical surface as a precursor to the theme.

11. When the first theme returns later in the movement, it does so without the introduction, which is standard. As a contemporary audience, we would not have expected to hear the introduction again, but in Beethoven, if something was important at the beginning of the symphony, it should still be important later.

12. When the opening theme returns, then, triumphantly and magnificently, a development of the introduction ensues. This development consists of a series of upward-resolving dissonances, rising for nearly two octaves, starting slowly and quietly, getting faster and faster, and ending, finally, quite thunderously. (**Musical selection**: Symphony No. 1 in C Major, Op. 21, movement 1, recap, theme 1 and introduction development.)

D. What conclusions can we draw from this miniscule look at Beethoven's First Symphony?

1. Despite its Haydnesque/Mozartian proportions, it is, in terms of its use of dissonance, thematic design, and expressive boldness, pure Beethoven.

2. Beethoven's so-called "Viennese" or "classical" compositional period, which includes Symphony Nos. 1 and 2, does not represent, as many sources have maintained, Beethoven's "learning of his craft" or his "assimilation of the classical style of Haydn and Mozart."

3. Beethoven was an original from the very beginning, and just how original he was capable of being would be revealed in three years with the composition of his Third Symphony.

VI. In 1801, Beethoven's career and finances were flourishing. His first symphony was a hit, his piano music was finding an ever-growing audience, and his first six quartets were quite popular.

    A. Unfortunately, he was in poor health. In particular, his loss of hearing, which began in 1796 and which he tried to keep hidden, was slowly becoming disabling. By 1818, he was completely deaf in his right ear and could hear only low-frequency sounds in his left.

    B. No one knows the actual cause of Beethoven's hearing loss and eventual deafness.

        1. Various specialists have advanced such diagnoses as calcification of the tiny bones of the ear (otoschlerosis), inflammation of the middle ear (otitis media), or disease of the inner ear (neuritis acoustica or labyrinthitus), conditions likely initiated by typhoid fever, which Beethoven probably contracted in 1787.

        2. Whatever the cause, Beethoven's hearing loss had a devastating impact on his ability to deal with the world. For years, Beethoven vacillated between panic, anxiety, hope, and depression, between optimism and pessimism.

        3. Beethoven's deepening emotional crisis over his hearing also seems to have inspired an extraordinary explosion of creativity.

        4. We might speculate that Beethoven's hearing disability was somehow linked to his creativity. Was the developing emotional crisis over his hearing a catalyst for his creativity and originality?

VII. The hearing crisis came to a head while Beethoven was staying in the village of Heiligenstadt—just north of Vienna, on the Danube—in October of 1802. We know this because of an extraordinary letter found among Beethoven's effects after he died.

    A. The Heiligenstadt Testament is an amazing confessional: part apology; part last will and testament; part suicide note; part rant and rave against God, humankind, and intractable fate. The Testament was written as an act of catharsis. Clearly, Beethoven needed to catalog his despair over his hearing loss; once written, the letter was filed away and left unsent.

B. By the fall of 1802, Beethoven's worst nightmares would seem to have become real. He was, again, isolated, enraged, and frustrated over the unfairness of "fate"; potentially the object of ridicule (as a deaf composer); perceived by those around him as being misanthropic; and worst of all, alone.

C. Beethoven wrote in the Heiligenstadt Testament, "So I must bid you farewell." It has been pointed out that the Heiligenstadt Testament is a leave-taking that also marks a new beginning, a fresh start.

D. In the Heiligenstadt Testament, Beethoven imagined his own death in order that he might be reborn. In doing so, he recreated himself in a new guise, self-sufficient and heroic.

    1. Some scholars have noted that the Heiligenstadt Testament is the literary prototype of the *Eroica* Symphony—a portrait of the artist as hero, stricken by deafness, withdrawn from humankind, conquering his impulses to suicide, struggling against fate, hoping to find "a single day of untroubled joy."

    2. It is a daydream compounded by heroism, death, and rebirth, a necessary step in Beethoven's subsequent reinvention of himself.

Lecture Seven
The Heroic Ideal

Scope: At the same time that Beethoven was writing the Heiligenstadt Testament, he was finishing the Symphony No. 2 in D Major, Op. 36, and preparing to reinvent himself in a new, heroic guise. His "model" for this new self-image was Napoleon Bonaparte, who represented a vision of individualism and empowerment. Beethoven later became disillusioned with Bonaparte, but held onto the sense of the individual struggling and triumphing against fate that Bonaparte had symbolized. Beethoven's Symphony No. 3 in Eb Major, Op. 55 (the *Eroica*), for example, was revolutionary in its expression of the heights and depths of the artist's emotions. Such music was based on Beethoven's beliefs that only dramatically conceived music could portray the full range of human experience and that the act of creating music was essentially self-expressive. With this symphony and other works of the period, Beethoven came to be known as a radical modernist who had broken forever with the classical standards of Haydn and Mozart.

Outline

I. Before we move on to Beethoven's so-called "heroic" music, we must note one last interesting fact about the Heiligenstadt Testament.

    A. Beethoven addressed the document as follows: "For my brothers Carl and ----- Beethoven."

    B. In fact, Beethoven went to great lengths throughout his life to avoid writing his younger brother's name, Johann.

    C. In refusing to write his brother's name, Beethoven was, in reality, refusing to write his father's name. Indeed, nowhere in any surviving document did Beethoven ever refer to his father by his first name.

II. In the fall of 1802, even as Beethoven was writing the Heiligenstadt Testament, he was finishing the fourth movement of his brilliant Symphony No. 2 in D Major, Op. 36.

A. True to form, when Beethoven was most depressed, he often wrote his most brilliant music, and the Second Symphony is no exception. (For an analysis of the grossly flatulent expressive content of the fourth movement of the Second Symphony—based as it is on Beethoven's own gastric problems—I invite you to listen to Lecture One of my Teaching Company course, *How to Listen to and Understand Great Music*, or Lecture Eight of *The Symphonies of Beethoven*.)

B. At the time, Beethoven was filled with suicidal despair even as he was poised at the edge of a personal and artistic reinvention; one suspects that the former was a necessary prerequisite for the latter.

C. In the fall of 1802, Beethoven-the-victim was about to reinvent himself as Beethoven-the-hero, a fighter struggling against his fate, overcoming the monsters and demons that would destroy him.

D. The "model" for Beethoven's heroic new self-image was Napoleon Bonaparte (1769–1821), who represented a vision of individual heroism and middle class empowerment.

III. On July 14, 1789, the French Revolution began. (**Musical selection**: Hector Berlioz, *La Marseillaise* (Rouget de Lisle), last verse [1830].)

A. Europe was galvanized by the event. Beethoven was eighteen-and-a-half years old when the French Revolution began, and he was flushed, inspired, and like most of his class, a bit frightened by the sense of inevitable change, personal liberty, and possible anarchy that the Revolution brought with it.

B. For Beethoven, the spirit of revolutionary change meant that nothing is forever, certainly not the Viennese classical style. Keep in mind, however, that Beethoven was not a political radical; he knew that he was supported by the Viennese aristocracy.

C. In 1799, the thirty-year-old Napoleon came to power, and with his rise, a vision of individualism and middle class heroism began to permeate the world of European arts, letters, and politics.

    1. Beethoven's personal identification with Napoleon went deeper still. Napoleon—as a Florentine among Corsicans and a Corsican among the French—was an outsider, who had accomplished and attained what he had as a result of his own power and vision.

> **2.** For Beethoven—a Rhinelander among the Viennese, hearing impaired among the hearing healthy, an alienated and angry man—Napoleon's image fit his own self-image perfectly.

D. By 1803, Napoleon seemed poised to bring the anti-monarchial, Enlightenment-inspired revolution to all of Europe. "Bonapartism" became the central political and philosophical issue of the post-Revolutionary period, and Napoleon was admired throughout Europe.

E. In 1803, Paris was the capital of the "new Europe" and the patronage capital of the world. Beethoven planned to move to Paris, where he thought he'd be more at home that he ever was in Vienna.

> **1.** He began the process of ingratiating himself into the Parisian musical scene. He dedicated his newest Sonata for Violin and Piano in A Major, Op. 47, to Rodolphe Kreutzer and Louis Adam, whom he called, "The first violinist and pianist in Paris." To this day, the piece is known as the "Kreutzer Sonata." (**Musical selection**: Sonata for Violin and Piano in A Minor, Op. 47, "Kreutzer," movement 3 [1803].)
>
> **2.** Beethoven also decided to write an opera with escape from tyranny as its theme, choosing a text called *Lenore* (which eventually became the opera *Fidelio*).
>
> **3.** Finally, Beethoven decided, almost certainly after the fact, to rename his just-completed Symphony No. 3 in Eb Major *Bonaparte*.
>
> **4.** According to Ferdinand Ries, when Napoleon declared himself emperor, however, Beethoven became enraged, predicting that Napoleon would become a tyrant. He changed the title of the symphony to *Eroica*.
>
> **5.** Beethoven's move to Paris was put on indefinite hold, a hold made permanent after Napoleon's attack on Austria in 1805.
>
> **6.** To the often-asked question of whether Beethoven's Symphony No. 3 is about Napoleon, the answer is: of course not. Napoleon was but the catalyst for Beethoven's emotional and compositional rebirth of 1804, much as Karl and Joanna would act as the catalysts for Beethoven's rebirth in 1819–1820.

7. If anything, Beethoven came to regard Napoleon as an authority figure, and he had a violent hatred toward such figures.
8. Further, in 1805, when Austria went to war with France, the Austrian Empire suffered worse defeats and more territorial losses than any other continental power during the Napoleonic Wars.

IV. Beethoven's Symphony No. 3 in Eb Major, Op. 55, the *Eroica*, received its public premiere on April 7, 1805.

A. The symphony begins with two proud and powerful Eb chords, which both ground the harmony and establish a martial and masculine mood. (**Musical selection at piano**: Symphony No. 3 in Eb Major, Op. 55, movement 1, opening chords.)

B. These opening chords are followed immediately by a lengthy theme in four phrases.
1. The opening theme in Eb Major is initially heard in the orchestral 'cellos, the "baritone" voice of the orchestra, which immediately imbues it with a masculine character and a certain expressive gravitas.
2. This opening theme is filled with both harmonic and rhythmic ambiguity. For example, just a few seconds in, the theme and its harmony take a sudden and dissonant turn toward the dark side of G Minor. (**Musical selection at piano**: Opening implication to G Minor via the C# in the bass.)
3. This C# is a dissonant musical element that carries with it the seeds of the dark side, of harmonic chaos and disruption; it is a character flaw in our otherwise confident theme.
4. The darkness it implies here at the beginning will be fully explored about halfway through this long and, in all ways, extraordinary opening movement.
5. About forty seconds in, the triple-meter beat that we have felt since the opening will momentarily seem to have switched to two—again, an unexpected ambiguity, an element that will, like the dissonance of the C#, be fully explored as we move through the movement.
6. This opening theme is obviously not standard fare. The theme is nothing less than a genuine "character," a person, replete with masculinity and serious character issues, a person that

carries within himself both the seeds of self-destruction and triumph. (**Musical selection**: Symphony No. 3 in Eb Major, Op. 55, movement 1, theme 1.)

    7. This instrumental theme has taken on the character of a rich and genuine personality. Beethoven's self-professed new path—his artistic rebirth in the guise of a hero—was nothing less than a recreation of the expressive nature of instrumental music, a reevaluation of the role of the artist as "creator," and a revolution in the nature of musical expression.

C. This first movement of Beethoven's Symphony No. 3 is nearly 700 measures long, about the length of any four-movement symphony by Haydn or Mozart. That first public performance in April of 1805 ran between fifty-five and sixty minutes; again, about twice the length of any symphony written to the time.

D. The expressive content, too, goes beyond anything anyone had ever heard in a concert hall: heights and depths of heroism, tragedy, joy, buffoonery, irony, and rage; these are words for the opera house, not the symphony hall.

E. Beethoven's Third is an instrumental work of operatic proportions, operatic expressive content, and dramatic, opera-like contrasts and conflicts. Beethoven had, before its composition, been thinking operatically.

    1. In March 1803, Beethoven completed his *Oratorio Christ on the Mount of Olives*, Op. 85 (Emanuel Schikeneder, librettist).

    2. From May 1803 to November 1803, Beethoven wrote the first draft of the *Eroica*.

    3. From late 1804 to the spring of 1806, Beethoven composed the opera *Fidelio* (which was started as *Lenore*).

F. Beethoven's "new path," his heroic reinvention of himself and his music in 1803, was based on two essential articles of faith.

    1. Instrumental music must also be "dramatic" music. Only dramatically conceived music filled with contrast, conflict, and ultimately, resolution can adequately portray the full range of human emotions and experience.

    2. The act of creating music is an essentially self-expressive act.

G. Nearly an hour after it begins, Beethoven's Third Symphony ends with an extraordinary affirmation of life and joy, as well as one of the longest final cadences in the repertoire. Listen to the conclusion of the symphony, the last minute of the fourth movement. (**Musical selection**: Symphony No. 3 in Eb Major, Op. 55, movement 4, conclusion.)

    H. Beethoven's contemporaries—his friends, enemies, and critics alike—did not understand the *Eroica*.

V. Critics found the symphony long and confusing. (For an in-depth analysis of the symphony and its reception, I direct you to Lectures Nine through Twelve of the Teaching Company course entitled *The Symphonies of Beethoven*.)

    A. We might not expect Beethoven's contemporaries to understand a piece of music as long, as personalized, as new, as different, and as violent and dissonant as the *Eroica*.

    B. Most great new music is critically panned after its premiere; what makes it new also precludes any contemporary audience from understanding it after only one hearing.

    C. Having said that, Beethoven's Third—the first of his so-called "Heroic Symphonies"—changed the history of Western music. It also marks Beethoven's musical rebirth and reinvention of himself, once again, in the face of terrific emotional and physical upheaval.

    D. In the Third Symphony, Beethoven found a compositional voice, an expressive temper, that allowed him to tap into his innermost emotions, his deepest fears, his longings, and his hopes.

        1. During his so-called "Heroic" compositional period, which spanned the years 1803–1812, Beethoven produced stunningly original masterworks at an amazing pace.

        2. In the seven-and-a-half years following the public premiere of the *Eroica*, Beethoven composed the Fourth, Fifth, Sixth, Seventh, and Eighth Symphonies; the Fourth and Fifth Piano Concerti; the Violin Concerto; the Triple Concerto; the five so-called middle string quartets; the *Choral Fantasy*; the *Leonore*, *Coriolan*, and *Egmont* Overtures; various violin and piano sonatas, songs, and arias; the Mass in C Major; and the opera *Fidelio*.

VI. Among the first works Beethoven composed immediately following the public premiere of the *Eroica* were the three String Quartets Op. 59, the so-called Razumovsky Quartets.

A. In 1805, Beethoven was commissioned to write three new string quartets for Count Andreas Kyrilovich Razumovsky, an amateur violinist and self-admitted string quartet enthusiast.

B. In commissioning the three new quartets, we might wonder what sort of music Count Razumovsky expected Beethoven to write.

    1. To answer that question, the Count looked at the six String Quartets of Op. 18, completed just six years before, in 1799.

    2. As we've discussed, the Op. 18 quartets would seem, on the surface at least, to be well within the classical style of Haydn and Mozart—tuneful, tasteful, accessible, and expressively restrained.

    3. The Count and his fellow musicians in his string quartet expected Beethoven to write similar music in 1805 and 1806. Let's listen to what he did write. (**Musical selection**: String Quartet No. 7 in F Major, Op. 59, No. 1, movement 1, ms. 1–52 [1806].)

    4. In this music, we hear a long, lyric, masculine theme, played initially by the 'cello, which has its parallel in the opening theme of the *Eroica* Symphony. We hear all sorts of solos for individual instruments and thematic material that is ripe with developmental possibilities. We also hear music that is, for us today, thoroughly entertaining and completely accessible. (**Musical selection:** String Quartet No. 7 in F Major, Op. 59, No. 1, Movement 1 [1806].)

    5. When the Count and his string quartet first played through this same music, they believed that Beethoven wanted to play a joke on them. The critical response to the Op. 59 quartets was no better.

    6. We listen to the last moment of the last movement of the third of the three Op. 59 quartets. (**Musical selection**: String Quartet No. 9 in C Major, Op. 59, No. 3, movement 4, conclusion.)

    7. With his Third Symphony and the String Quartets Op. 59, Beethoven came to be regarded as a radical modernist, a composer of powerful and dangerous music, and a revolutionary whose music would seem to have broken forever with the classical standards and civility of Haydn and Mozart.

VII. Typically, tremendous emotional stress for Beethoven led to a proactive compositional stance.

    A. In 1803, he reinvented himself musically and emerged from depression with a vision of himself as a hero triumphing over fate and with a belief that his music must be a vehicle for self-expression.

    B. In reinventing himself and his art, Beethoven changed forever the nature and content of Western music.

Lecture Eight
Two Concerts, 1808 and 1824

Scope: A long and difficult concert in December 1808 marked Beethoven's final assault on classicism. In it, he premiered the Fifth and Sixth Symphonies, among other pieces, to an exhausted and critical audience, but one that would ultimately come to appreciate the musical genius and explosive spirit of his work. From that point on, Beethoven became a legend. More than fifteen years later, in May 1824, another concert was arranged, to premiere the Ninth Symphony. The reception, this time, was overwhelming, and the Ninth has come to be regarded as the most important piece of music composed in the 19th century. The Ninth embodies Beethoven's belief that the expressive needs of the artist must transcend the time-honored assumptions of art. During this time, Beethoven was consumed by his craft, dedicating the last two-and-a-half years of his life to composing string quartets. In November 1826, Beethoven fell ill with cirrhosis of the liver and died on March 26, 1827. In the end, he had managed a reconciliation with his family and was given an affectionate tribute by the Viennese people.

Outline

I.   Beethoven changed forever the expressive language of Western music, as well as the template for the role of the composer.

  A. The musicologist Donald Grout wrote, "Beethoven was one of the great disruptive forces in the history of music. After him, nothing could ever be the same again; he had opened the gateway to a new world."

  B. As we begin this last lecture on Beethoven, we must ask a difficult, yet extremely important question: Was Beethoven a better and more original composer as a result of his hearing loss, as a result of the spiritual and physical isolation he suffered?

  C. Maynard Solomon proposes this answer: "In his increasingly deaf world, Beethoven could experiment with new forms of experience, free of the external environment; free from the rigidities of the material world; free, like the dreamer, to combine and recombine the stuff of reality, in accordance with his desires, into previously undreamed-of forms and structures."

D. And "dream of music" Beethoven did. Between 1806 and 1808, one masterwork after another rolled out of his studio: the String Quartets Op. 59; the Fourth, Fifth, and Sixth Symphonies; the Violin Concerto; the Fourth Piano Concerto; the *Choral Fantasy*, Op. 80; the Mass in C Major, Op. 86, to name just a few.

II. Beethoven got the opportunity to present this music in December 1808, when he was given the use of the Theater an der Wien for what was then called an *Akademie*, or benefit concert.

A. Beethoven had experienced problems with the players at this theater in the past, and the program he put together for the concert was exceedingly long and difficult. In fact, it was impossible to go through a single full rehearsal of all the pieces to be performed before the concert.

B. Beethoven was particularly worried about the premiere of his new C Minor Symphony (No. 5).

1. The symphony was originally scheduled to be performed at the end of the concert, and Beethoven was concerned that, by then, both the performers and the audience would be exhausted. His solution was to add more music after the premiere of the Fifth.

2. According to his student Carl Czerny, "He chose a song which he had composed many years earlier, planned the variations, the chorus, etc. Thus originated the Choral Fantasy [Op. 80]. It was finished so late that it could scarcely be sufficiently rehearsed."

3. During the performance of *Choral Fantasy*, Beethoven, at the piano, forgot his own instructions about some repetitions and, as a result, the *Fantasy* actually got one-and-a-half performances, making the evening even longer!

C. The evening began with the premiere of the Symphony No. 6 in F Major, Op. 68. (**Musical selection**: Symphony No. 6 in F Major, Op. 68, movement 1 opening [1808].)

D. The Sixth Symphony went well enough, but the next piece did not go well, the premiere of *Ah Perfido*, Scene and Aria, Op. 65. (**Musical selection**: *Ah Perfido*, Scene and Aria, Op. 65 [1796].)

E. Next on the concert came the premiere of the Kyrie and Gloria from the Mass in C Major, Op. 86. (**Musical selection**: Mass in C Major, Op. 86, Kyrie [1807].)

F. The first half of the concert ended with the public premiere of the Piano Concerto No. 4 in G Major, Op. 58, with Beethoven as soloist. (**Musical selection**: Piano Concerto No. 4 in G Major, Op. 58, movement 1, opening [1806].)

G. The second half of the concert began with the premiere of the Fifth Symphony; to say that this wild, vaguely heavy-metal–sounding music fell on stunned and uncomprehending ears is an understatement. (**Musical selection**: Symphony No. 5 in C Minor, Op. 67, movement 1 [1808].)

H. Next came the premiere of the Sanctus from the Mass in C Major. (**Musical selection**: Mass in C Major, Op. 86, Sanctus [1807].)

I. Next, Beethoven improvised a piano fantasy and, finally, the concert ended with the premiere of the *Choral Fantasy* Op. 80 for Piano, Orchestra, and Chorus.

J. Was this concert a fiasco? Yes. Yet it remains one of the most famous in the history of Western music. If nothing else, it marks Beethoven's final assault on classicism. After this concert—with the premieres of the Fifth and Sixth Symphonies—the Beethoven legend truly began to grow.

III. If Beethoven's music was so rough and harsh, so beyond his audience's ability to like and comprehend it, why was his music so popular? Why did his career thrive?

    A. First, the true musical connoisseurs of Vienna recognized the genius, power, and truth of Beethoven's music almost immediately. They didn't listen to Beethoven's music for "entertainment" any more than today's connoisseur looks to modern art for pretty pictures and calming, idealized imagery.

        1. These Viennese connoisseurs were, to their credit, willing and able to support Beethoven, leaving him pretty much alone to write what he chose.

        2. For example, in 1809, to ensure Beethoven's continued residence in Vienna, Prince Lobkowitz, Prince Kinsky, and Archduke Rudolf created a 4,000-florin annuity to be paid to Beethoven, provided he stayed in Austria.

B. The second reason for the great popularity of Beethoven's "Heroic" music during the first decade of the 18th century was that this music offered a sense of national pride for an Austrian nation that had been defeated by the French a number of times between 1797–1809.

C. Third, the musical public of Europe heard in Beethoven's music a power and relevance that mirrored the dangerous and explosive spirit of the time. Again, no one found Goya's art "pretty," but Beethoven's music, like Goya's art, expressed and crystallized truths that, though often painful, cut to the spirit of the time.

IV. Sometime during the early months of 1824, Beethoven received a letter signed by thirty of the leading musicians, publishers, and music connoisseurs of Vienna. The co-signers of the letter had heard that Beethoven was nearing completion of a Ninth Symphony and were eager to make sure that its premiere would take place in Vienna.

A. After some delay, a concert date and place were set for the premiere of Beethoven's Symphony No. 9. Twelve years had elapsed between the completion of the Eighth and Ninth Symphonies, fully as much time as there had been between the First and the Eighth.

B. The date was May 7, 1824, more than fifteen years after the premiere of the Fifth and Sixth Symphonies at the Theater an der Wien. The location was the Karntnertor Theater in Vienna, and the conditions were excellent. The orchestra and chorus were well rehearsed, and an atmosphere of electricity filled the sold-out hall.

C. The program included *Consecration of the House Overture*, Op. 124 (premiere); Kyrie, Credo, and Agnus Dei from the *Missa Solemnis*, Op. 123; and Symphony No. 9 in D Minor, Op. 125 (premiere).

D. During the performance of the Ninth, Beethoven stood near the chorus, looking on in his score, and beating time with his hand. The conductor warned the chorus not to look at him during the performance; as we know, one of the singers turned the deaf Beethoven around so that he might see the extraordinary ovation that followed the conclusion of the piece. (**Musical selection**: Symphony No. 9 in D Minor, Op. 125, movement 4, conclusion [1824].)

E. Beethoven's Symphony No. 9 was the most influential and important piece of music composed in the 19th century. It also rendered insignificant time-honored distinctions that had provided the essential foundation for genre in Western music: the distinction between "abstract" and "literary" music; between religious and secular music; and between symphony and opera, cantata, oratorio, and song.

F. By its example, Beethoven's Ninth said to the next generations of composers that something as basic as genre is contextual: The expressive needs and desires of the artist must transcend, must take precedence over, any convention, no matter how sacred, time honored, or popular that convention may be.

V. During his last years, Beethoven was completely consumed by his craft. He also remained a cantankerous and difficult character to the end, fighting constantly with producers and friends over money, going through housekeepers at an alarming rate, and being downright dishonest in his dealings with publishers.

   A. The last two-and-a-half years of Beethoven's compositional life were dedicated entirely to composing string quartets. Never before had he concentrated for so long on a single genre of music.
      1. The results were the so-called late string quartets Op. 127, Op. 130, Op. 131, Op. 132, Op. 135, and the *Grosse* ("Grand") *Fugue*, Op. 133.
      2. These late quartets constitute a genre of music unto themselves; they are so varied, so different, so new that they defy easy description.

   B. The first of the late string quartets, the Quartet in Eb Major, Op. 127, was composed in large part during the second half of 1824, immediately after the premiere of the Ninth Symphony.
      1. If a string quartet can be both symphonic and operatic in scope, then it is Op. 127.
      2. In Op. 127, we are witness to passages of great symphonic majesty and magnificence, as well as the sort of lyricism, dramatic conflicts and resolutions, tensions and revelations that we ordinarily associate with the operatic stage. (**Musical selection**: String Quartet in Eb Major, Op. 127, movement 1 [1824].)

C. The last piece of music Beethoven completed was a new final movement for the String Quartet in Bb, Op. 130.

   1. The original last movement of the Op. 130 quartet, completed in November 1825, was a huge and virtuosic fugue. (**Musical selection**: *Grosse Fugue* in Bb Major, Op. 133.)

   2. After finishing the quartet in Bb, Op. 130, Beethoven decided to publish the fugue as a self-standing piece, the *Grosse Fugue*, Op. 133.

   3. In its place, Beethoven composed a shorter, simpler movement in Bb, which he then plugged into the quartet. This "new" final movement for Op. 130 is the last music Beethoven ever wrote. (**Musical selection**: String Quartet in Bb, Op. 130, movement 6.)

D. By the time he finished this "replacement" movement, in late November 1826, Beethoven was already ill. He had only four more months to live.

VI. In 1824, Beethoven's relationship with his nephew Karl was disintegrating.

   A. At this time, Beethoven, terrified that Karl might be having "relations" with women (and, in those days of rampant syphilis, exposed to mortal "dangers"), hired an investigator to follow Karl.

   B. In November 1824, Karl and Beethoven got into such a fight that Beethoven's landlady served notice of his eviction. By spring of 1825, Beethoven was convinced that Karl was seeing his mother again, and that this was the root of Karl's behavioral problems.

   C. The climax of this dispute occurred in August 1826. Karl, twenty years old and being followed by Beethoven's man Karl Holz, pawned his watch, bought two pistols, wrote suicide notes—one to Beethoven and one to his best friend, Joseph Niemetz—climbed a mountain, put one of the guns to his head, and shot himself.

   D. He didn't die. Karl hadn't put enough powder in the gun and had held it at too sharp an angle when he put it to his head. The bullet lodged fairly harmlessly in his scalp. He was rescued by a passerby and taken, at his request, to his mother's house.

   E. The suicide attempt was the last step in Karl's separation of himself from Beethoven. During the fall of 1826, Karl finally escaped the clutches of his uncle by joining the army, after which he became a minor official in the Austrian bureaucracy. We are told that he lived a useful, middle-class, and apparently contented existence.

F. Karl's suicide attempt came as a terrible blow to Beethoven. During the fall of 1826, in the months following the attempt, Beethoven began suffering alarming symptoms, including diarrhea; a painful, swollen belly; constant thirst and loss of appetite; and painfully swollen feet.

G. In early December, Beethoven came down with pneumonia. By mid-December, Beethoven was mortally ill. The diagnosis was cirrhosis of the liver. (Beethoven was not an alcoholic but had almost certainly inherited a genetic predisposition to cirrhosis.)

H. It was a painful and slow death, slow enough for Beethoven to know what was happening to him and slow enough for him to make some amends. He left all his property to Karl and reconciled himself to both of his sisters-in-law.

I. The end came on March 26. Of all people, Johanna van Beethoven, alone, was by his side. As snow fell and a violent thunderstorm raged outside, Beethoven suddenly opened his eyes, lifted his right hand, and clenched it into a fist. When his hand fell back to the bed, Beethoven was dead.

J. Between 10,000 and 30,000 Viennese crowded the street to witness Beethoven's funeral procession. The Viennese poet Franz Grillparzer wrote the funeral oration. The Viennese, who always enjoy a lovely funeral, enjoyed this one; it was, by all accounts, a great party.

K. In fact, the funeral was quite a contrast with the conditions in which Beethoven spent the last years of his life. When Gioacchino Rossini met Beethoven in 1822, he was stunned by the squalor of Beethoven's apartment and the sadness of the artist himself. As Frances Toye tells the story, "Later, he [Rossini] tried to do something for Beethoven, himself heading a subscription list. To no purpose, however. The answer [the Viennese gave] was always the same: 'Beethoven is impossible'" (Scherman/Biancolli).

Timeline

1770 ....Beethoven is born in Bonn on December 17.

1789 ....Beethoven successfully petitions the Elector of Bonn to grant the Beethoven brothers half their father's pension and to have their father removed from Bonn.

1792 ....Beethoven departs Bonn for Vienna, Austria, in November.

1796 ....Beethoven's slow hearing loss begins.

1800 ....Symphony No. 1 is premiered on April 2.

1802 ....Beethoven writes the Heiligenstadt Testament in October.

1803 ....Symphony No. 2 is premiered on April 5.

1805 ....The Eroica Symphony is premiered on April 7.

1807 ....Symphony No. 4 is premiered on March 5.

1808 ....Symphony Nos. 5 and 6 are premiered on December 22.

1809 ....Archduke Rudolph and Princes Lobkowitz and Kinsky sign a contract of lifetime support for Beethoven.

1812 ....Beethoven breaks off his love affair with Antonie Brentano.

1813 ....Symphony No. 7 is premiered on December 8.

1814 .... Beethoven gives his last public performance as a pianist. He is enjoying a sudden increase in his popularity. Symphony No. 8 is premiered on February 4.

1815 .... Beethoven falls out of favor with the public. His hearing suffers another rapid deterioration. His patrons are leaving Vienna or are estranged from him. He is increasingly regarded as insane. His brother Casper dies and he begins litigation to gain custody of his nephew Karl.

1824 .... Symphony No. 9 is premiered on May 7.

1827 .... Beethoven dies on March 26.

Glossary

academy: Public concert in 18th century Vienna, Austria.

arpeggio: Chord broken up into consecutively played notes.

augmented: (1) Major or perfect interval extended by a semi-tone, e.g., augmented sixth: C-A sharp. (2) Notes that are doubled in value; e.g., a quarter note becomes a half note. Augmentation is a device for heightening the drama of a musical section by extenuating the note values of the melody.

Baroque: Sixteenth- and 17th-century artistic style characterized by extreme elaboration. In music, the style was marked by the complex interplay of melodies, as manifest, for example, in a fugue.

bridge: Musical passage linking one section or theme to another.

cadence: Short harmonic formulas that close a musical section or movement. The commonest formula is dominant–tonic (V–I). (1) A closed (or perfect) cadence fully resolves: The dominant is followed by the expected tonic. (2) An open (or imperfect) cadence is a temporary point of rest, usually on an unresolved dominant. (3) A deceptive (or interrupted) cadence is one in which the dominant resolves to some chord other than the expected tonic.

cadenza: Passage for solo instrument in an orchestral work, usually a concerto, designed to showcase the player's skills.

chromatic: Scale in which all the pitches are present. On a keyboard, this translates as moving consecutively from white notes to black notes.

Classical: Designation given to works of art of the 17th and 18th centuries, characterized by clear lines and balanced form.

coda: Section of music that brings a sonata-allegro movement to a close.

crescendo: Getting louder.

da capo: Back to the top, or beginning (instruction in a score).

development: Section in a classical sonata-allegro movement in which the main themes are developed.

diminished: Minor or perfect interval that is reduced by one semi-tone; e.g., minor seventh, C-B flat, becomes diminished when the minor is reduced by one semi-tone to become C sharp-B flat. Diminished sevenths are extremely unstable harmonies that can lead in a variety of harmonic directions.

dissonance: Unresolved and unstable interval or chord.

dominant: Fifth note of a scale and the key of that note; e.g., G is the dominant of C. The second theme in a classical sonata-allegro exposition first appears in the dominant.

double fugue: Complex fugue with two subjects, or themes.

drone: Note or notes, usually in the bass, sustained throughout a musical section or composition; characteristic of bagpipe music.

dynamics: Degrees of loudness, e.g., *piano* (quiet), *forte* (loud), indicated in a musical score.

enharmonic: Notes that are identical in sound, but with different spellings, depending on the key context, e.g., C sharp and D flat.

Enlightenment: 18th century philosophical movement characterized by rationalism and positing that individuals are responsible for their own destinies and all men are born equal.

Eroica: Sobriquet, literally meaning "heroic," given to Beethoven's Symphony No. 3.

exposition: Section in a classical sonata-allegro movement in which the main themes are exposed, or introduced.

fermata: Pause.

forte: Loud.

French overture: Invented by the French composer Jean Baptiste Lully, court composer to King Louis XIV. The French Overture was played at the theater to welcome the king and to set the mood for the action on the stage. It is characterized by its grandiose themes; slow, stately tempo; dotted rhythms; and sweeping scales.

fugato: Truncated fugue in which the exposition is not followed by true development.

fugue: Major, complex Baroque musical form, distantly related to the round, in which a theme (or subject) is repeated at different pitch levels in succession and is developed by means of various contrapuntal techniques.

Gesamtkunstwerk: All-inclusive artwork or art form, containing music, drama, poetry, dance, and so on; term coined by Richard Wagner.

Heiligenstadt Testament: Confessional document penned by Beethoven at a time of extreme psychological crisis. In it, he despairs over his realization that he is going deaf but determines to soldier on.

hemiola: Temporary use of a displaced accent to produce a feeling of changed meter. Beethoven uses it to effect an apparent change from triple (3/4) meter to duple (2/4) meter, without actually changing the meter.

home key: Main key of a movement or composition.

homophonic: A musical passage or piece that has one main melody and everything else is accompaniment.

interval: Distance in pitch between two tones, e.g., C-G (upwards) = a fifth.

inversion: Loosely applied to indicate a reversal in direction; e.g., a melody that goes up, goes down in inversion and vice versa. Its strict definitions are as follows: (1) Harmonic inversion: The bottom note of an interval, or chord, is transferred to its higher octave, or its higher note is transferred to its lower octave; e.g., C-E-G (played together) becomes E-G-C or E-C-G. (2) Melodic inversion: An ascending interval (one note played after the other) is changed to its corresponding descending interval and vice versa; e.g., C-D-E becomes C-B-A.

K. numbers: Koechel numbers, named after L. von Koechel, are a cataloging identification attached to works by Mozart.

measure: Metric unit; space between two bar lines.

melisma: Tightly wound, elaborate melodic line.

meter: Rhythmic measure, e.g., triple meter (3/4) in which there are three beats to the bar, or duple meter (2/4) in which there are two beats to the bar.

metric modulation: Main beat remains the same while the rhythmic subdivisions change. This alters the meter without disturbing the tempo.

minuet: 17th- and 18th-century, graceful and dignified dance in moderately slow three-quarter time.

minuet and trio: Form of a movement (usually the third) in a classical symphony. The movement is in ternary (ABA) form with the first minuet repeated after the trio and each section itself repeated.

modal ambiguity: Harmonic ambiguity, in which the main key is not clearly identified.

mode: Major or minor key (in modern Western usage).

modulation: Change from one key to another.

motive: Short musical phrase that can be used as a building block in compositional development.

movement: Independent section within a larger work.

musette: (1) Bagpipe common in Europe in the 17th and 18th centuries. (2) Piece of music in rustic style with a drone bass.

musical form: Overall formulaic structure of a composition, e.g., sonata form; also the smaller divisions of the overall structure, such as the development section.

ostinato: Motive that is repeated over and over again.

overture: Music that precedes an opera or play.

pedal note: Pitch sustained for a long period of time against which other changing material is played. A pedal harmony is a sustained chord serving the same purpose.

piano: Soft or quiet.

piano trio: Composition for piano, violin, and cello.

pivot modulation: A tone common to two chords is used to effect a smooth change of key. For example, F sharp-A-C sharp (F sharp minor triad) and F-A-C (F major triad) have A in common. This note can serve as a pivot to swing the mode from F sharp minor to F major.

pizzicato: Very short (plucked) notes.

polyphony: Dominant compositional style of the preclassical era, in which multiple melodies are played together (linear development), as opposed to one melody played with harmonic accompaniment.

quartet: (1) Ensemble of four instruments. (2) Piece for four instruments.

recapitulation: Section following the development in a sonata-allegro movement, in which the main themes return in their original form.

recitative: Operatic convention in which the lines are half sung, half spoken.

retrograde: Backwards.

retrograde inversion: Backwards and upside down.

ritardando: Gradually getting slower (abbreviation: *ritard*).

scherzo: "Joke"; name given by Beethoven and his successors to designate a whimsical, often witty, fast movement in triple time.

semi-tone: Smallest interval in Western music; on the keyboard, the distance between a black note and a white note; also, B-C and E-F.

sequence: Successive repetitions of a motive at different pitches. A compositional technique for extending melodic ideas.

sonata-allegro form (also known as sonata form): Most important musical structure of the classical era. It is based on the concept of dramatic interaction between two contrasting themes and structured in four parts, sometimes with an introduction to the exposition or first part. The exposition introduces the main themes that will be developed in the development section. The themes return in the recapitulation section and the movement is closed with a coda.

stringendo: Compressing time; getting faster.

string quartet: (1) Ensemble of four stringed instruments: two violins, viola, and cello. (2) Composition for such an ensemble.

symphony: Large-scale instrumental composition for orchestra, containing several movements. The Viennese classical symphony usually had four movements.

syncopation: Displacement of the expected accent from a strong beat to a weak beat and vice versa.

theme and variations: Musical form in which a theme is introduced, then treated to a series of variations on some aspect of that theme.

tonic: First note of the scale; main key of a composition or musical section.

transition (or bridge): Musical passage linking two sections.

triad: Chord consisting of three notes: the root, the third, and the fifth, e.g., C-E-G, the triad of C major.

trio: (1) Ensemble of three instruments. (2) Composition for three instruments. (3) Type of minuet, frequently rustic in nature and paired with another minuet to form a movement in a classical-era symphony.

triplet: Three notes occurring in the space of one beat.

tutti: Whole orchestra plays together.

Viennese Classical Style: Style that dominated European music in the late 18th century. It is characterized by clarity of melodies, harmonies, and rhythms and balanced, proportional musical structures.

voice: A pitch or register, commonly used to refer to the four melodic pitches: soprano, alto, tenor, and bass.

Biographical Notes

Beethoven, Casper Anton Carl van (1774–1815). Beethoven's brother, who married Johanna Reiss. Beethoven would later claim custody of their son Karl.

Beethoven, Johann van (1740?–1792). Beethoven's father; musician and teacher.

Beethoven, Maria Magdalena van (1746–1787). Beethoven's mother.

Beethoven, Nikolaus Johann van (1776–1848). Beethoven's brother; apothecary.

Brentano, Antonie (1780–1869). Wife of Franz Brentano. Antonie was the "Immortal Beloved," the great love of Beethoven's life.

Kinsky, Prince Ferdinand (1781–1812). Co-donor of Beethoven's annuity.

Lichnowsky, Prince Karl (1756–1814). Major patron of Beethoven.

Lobkowitz, Prince Josef (1772–1816). Patron, admirer, and co-donor of Beethoven's annuity; major figure in the Austro-Hungarian Empire.

Maezel, Johannes Nepomuk (1772–1838). Inventor of the metronome and other mechanical instruments. The battle symphony (*Wellington's Victory*) was his idea.

Neefe, Christian (1748–1798). Composer who introduced Beethoven to the works of Johann Sebastian Bach.

Rasoumovsky, Prince Andrei (1752–1836). Patron and friend of Beethoven. Rasoumovsky was the Russian ambassador in Vienna and one of the wealthiest and most brilliant men in Europe.

Ries, Ferdinand (1784–1838). Pianist and composer. Ries was a student of Beethoven and later his friend. One of Beethoven's earliest biographers.

Rudolph, Archduke of Austria (1788–1832). Son of Leopold II. Rudolph was a student of Beethoven and one of the three donors of Beethoven's annuity.

Schindler, Anton (1795–1864). Violinist and conductor. Schindler was a devoted friend of Beethoven and an early biographer.

Spohr, Ludwig (1784–1859). Violinist, composer, and conductor. He wrote an autobiography that contains anecdotes about Beethoven.

Bibliography

Anderson, Emily, ed. and trans. *The Letters of Beethoven*. Macmillan, London, 1966.

Barea, Ilse. *Vienna*. Knopf, New York, 1966.

Fischer, Gottfried, edited by Joseph Schmidt-Gorg. *Remembering Beethoven's Youth*. Beethovenhaus, Bonn, 1971.

Forbes, Elliot. *Thayer's Life of Beethoven*. Princeton University Press, Princeton, 1964; revised edition 1967.

Freud, Sigmund. *The Ego and the Id*, Volume 19, standard edition.

Glover, Edward. *On the Early Development of Mind*. Imago, London, 1956.

Grout, Donald, and Palisca, Claude. *A History of Western Music*, fourth edition. W. W. Norton, New York, 1988.

Grove, George. *Beethoven and His Nine Symphonies*. Dover, New York, 1962 (originally published 1898).

Herriot, Edouard. *The Life and Times of Beethoven*. Macmillan, New York, 1935.

Hamburger, Michael. *Beethoven, Letters, Journals and Conversations*. Thames and Hudson, New York, 1951.

Hopkins, Antony. *The Nine Symphonies of Beethoven*. Heineman, London, 1981.

Kerman, Joseph. *The Beethoven Quartets.* Alfred A. Knopf, New York, 1971.

Kerst, Friedrich, ed. *Die Erinnerungen an Beethoven*. Julius Hoffman, Stuttgart, 1913.

Kinderman, William. *Beethoven*. University of California Press, Berkeley, 1995.

Landon, H. C. Robbins. *Beethoven*. Macmillan, New York, 1970.

Magazin der Muzik. C. F. Cramer, ed. Volume 1, p. 394.

Neumayr, Anton. *Music and Medicine*. Medi-Ed Press, Bloomington, 1994.

Palmer, Robert, and Colton, Joel. *A History of the Modern World*. Alfred A. Knopf, New York, 1984.

Scherman, Thomas, and Biancolli, Louis, eds. *The Beethoven Companion*. Doubleday, New York, 1972.

Schindler, Anton. *Beethoven as I Knew Him*. University of North Carolina Press, Chapel Hill, 1966.

Schom, Alan. *Napoleon Bonaparte*. Harper Collins, New York, 1997.

Schonberg, Harold. *The Great Pianists*. Simon and Schuster, New York, 1963.

———. *The Lives of the Great Composers*. W. W. Norton, New York, 1970.

Solomon, Maynard. *Beethoven*. Schirmer, New York, 1998.

———. *Beethoven Essays*. Harvard University Press, Cambridge, 1988.

Sonneck, O. G. *Beethoven: Impressions of Contemporaries*. Schirmer, New York, 1926.

Steinberg, Michael. "San Francisco Symphony Program Note," June 15, 1989.

Steiner, George. *Tolstoy or Dostoevsky*. Vintage, New York, 1961.

Sterba, Edith, and Sterba, Richard. *Beethoven and His Nephew*. Pantheon, New York, 1954.

Thayer, Alexander; Dieters, Hermann; and Riemann, Hugo. *Ludwig van Beethoven's Life*. Breitkopf and Hartel, Leipzig, 1923.

Wegeler, Franz, and Ries, Ferdinand. *Beethoven Remembered*. Bonn, revised 1972.

Winter, Robert, and Martin, Robert. *The Beethoven Quartet Companion*. University of California Press, Berkeley, 1994.

Acknowledgments

Professor Greenberg quotes excerpts from the following publications:

Beethoven, H.C. Robbins Landon. Copyright 1972.
Used by permission of Thames and Hudson, Ltd., London, UK.

The Beethoven Companion, Thomas K. Scherman and Louis Biancolli,
Copyright 1972 by Thomas K. Scherman and Louis Biancolli.
Used by permission of Doubleday, a division of Random House, Inc.

Notes